UNITY, FREEDOM & PEACE

A Blueprint for Tomorrow

UNITY, FREEDOM & PEACE

A Blueprint for Tomorrow

— by —

Nelson A. Rockefeller

 RANDOM HOUSE

NEW YORK

ACKNOWLEDGMENTS

The author wishes to acknowledge the assistance of Rodney Campbell, Hugh Morrow, Mary McAniff and Nancy Shea in editorial consultation, research and development; of Mary Nestor, Dean McIlnay and Marshall Watzke in administrative duties; of T. Norman Hurd, Henry A. Kissinger, Jonathan Moore, Oscar M. Ruebhausen and William Watts in the reading of the manuscript and contribution of ideas. He also extends his thanks to Cornell Capa for the use of the jacket photograph—and to C. A. Wimpfheimer, James Silberman and Sally Kovalchick of Random House, Inc.

v

CONTENTS

UNITY,

FREEDOM

& PEACE

A Blueprint for Tomorrow

4598

I

THE LIGHT OF
HIGH RESOLVE

One of my heroes is Theodore Roosevelt, the twenty-sixth President of the United States. What a man he was—and what a fabulous, zestful life he led! An asthmatic, puny child, he steeled his strength and his spirit and won lightweight boxing contests and election to Phi Beta Kappa at Harvard University. He was a cattle rancher in North Dakota, a police commissioner and social reformer in New York City. In the Spanish-American War, he led the legendary Rough Riders in their famous charge up San Juan Hill outside Santiago in Cuba. But it was as President that his vision, his judgment and his professional sense of good management became dominant in his character. Theodore Roosevelt saw that our country—then as now—was divided, unsure of itself, and plagued with antagonisms and bitterness. So he set forth in quest of unity, freedom and peace.

"We, here in America," he said, "hold in our hands the hope of the world, the fate of the coming years; and shame and disgrace will be ours if, in our eyes, the light of high resolve is dimmed, if we trail in the dust the golden hopes of men."

This year—my twenty-eighth year in federal and state government service and my tenth as Governor of New York—I announced my active candidacy for the Presidency in the same quest for unity, freedom and peace.

I did this because, first of all, the dramatic and unprecedented events of our recent history have revealed in most serious terms the gravity of the crisis that we face as a people. Secondly, in the new circumstances that confront the nation, I found that to comment from the sidelines was not an effective way to present the alternatives of policy and leadership that I believe essential to order and progress at home and to peace and understanding abroad. Thirdly, I was deeply disturbed by the course of events, the growing unrest and anxiety at home and the signs of disintegration abroad. Very simply, I concluded that I could best serve my country by taking this course at this time.

There can be no question that the United States is in serious difficulties: The war in Vietnam. The attack on the dollar. The assassination of Martin Luther King. The riots. The racial confrontation. The escalating costs and enervating failures of the war against poverty. Crime. The pollution crisis. Strategic misconceptions in the Pentagon and muddled purposes in the State Department. The polarization of too many Americans into political positions of the left and the right. The isolation of business from public affairs. The alienation of youth.

Yet Theodore Roosevelt, facing comparably serious times, maintained a calm faith in our institutions.

"I preach the gospel of hope," he said, "of resolution and confident belief in the destiny of this mighty Republic."

I, too, believe that we will enter our own time of testing—and surmount our new challenges—and unify our people—and advance the cause of freedom—and achieve peace with justice in the world.

We have been learning, often in harsh, cruel ways, that there is no substitute for capable leadership. We have been shown that we cannot wage our wars, educate our young, aid our needy, expand our armies, retrain our unemployed, rebuild our cities, cleanse our waters and confound our enemies all at one frenzied moment. We have learned that by diffusing our purposes and scattering our resources—without priority and without precision— we have come to seem too often a nation desperately trying at almost everything while totally triumphing at very little.

And yet, before the world, America is not just a power: it is a promise. It is not enough for our country to be extraordinary in might; it must be exemplary in meaning. Our honor and our role in the world finally depend on the living proof that we are a just society. This means a society that can elevate its own purposes, unite its own people, and solve its own problems. This also means that we need to understand our own history and how vital it is—never more so than now—to all men who are free and all men who long to be free.

How closely we are watched, and how carefully we are analyzed! "You are advancing in the night, bearing torches toward which mankind would be glad to turn, but you have no universal ideas to communicate." Thus one French critic. Or: "I sought for the greatness and genius of America in her commodious harbors and her ample rivers, in her fertile fields and boundless forests, in her rich mines and her vast world commerce, in her democratic Congress and matchless Constitution—and it was not there. America is great because America is good— and if America ever ceases to be good—America will cease to be great." That from another philosophical visitor.

"Since America was born and brought up with this sense of universal import," wrote Russell Davenport, "this generation of Americans has a duty either to renounce it or reaffirm it in a way that is clear both to ourselves and to mankind." President Washington said that liberty— and self-government—were *"finally* staked on the experiment entrusted to the hands of the American people." President Adams called our country "that grand scheme and design in Providence," and President Lincoln termed our experiment in freedom "the germ which has vegetated, and still is to grow and expand into the universal liberty of mankind." President Theodore Roosevelt translated all this into the specific administration of a modern state with the special vigor that we need—and must have—today. Ponder his wisdom and listen to his roar:

"The most timid rabbit alive is not afraid of a dead issue. It is only the live issues that make timid politicians run away and crooked politicians walk crookedly. It does not need any courage to take the right stand against slavery and secession when we speak of Lincoln, for the excellent reason that both slavery and secession are dead. But it takes real courage to apply Lincoln's teachings to the industrial and political conditions of the day. And therefore only a man with some stuff in him will make the effort."

What, then, must be the ruling spirit of this moment? First, we need to assimilate and interpret some of the stern truths we face. We shall swiftly bring our Gross National Product above the historic $850 billion level—but some thirty million of our people still live in poverty, insecurity and fear. Two-thirds of these are white and one-third are black. To put it in another, sharper way, 12 percent of white Americans and 41 percent of black Americans are not sharing in our ways of life, our American dream. Infant mortality rates are actually higher in the United States than in ten other nations, especially among our Negro citizens.

I am well aware there has been an explosion of constitutional and legal progress with regard to the protection of civil rights. But I have always thought it a matter of fact, not opinion, that the most promising way to solve the race crisis in America is pragmatic. Offer the opportunities, of jobs, education, housing, medical care, leisure, the specif-

ics of the American dream, if you will—and a true sharing
of our American experience will follow. Private enterprise
is infinitely better equipped than government to enhance
these opportunities while government is fitted to provide
incentives, and to underwrite human concerns. What we
need, really, in dealing with this situation is the drive and
dynamism of a true partnership, a true unity, through
which the goodwill and creativity of our people can make
themselves felt.

Let no one forget that we started all this—that the American example of freedom and a free government, dedicated
to lifting the burdens from the shoulders of men, is an in-
spiration today as always to others in distant lands who
seek a better life. Those of us who have worked abroad are
familiar with the legend scrawled on the walls of other
continents: "Yankee go home—and take me with you." Let
no one forget that it is the system of individual initiative
and private enterprise that has kept us free, made us the
world's most powerful nation, and brought most of the
American people to the highest standard of living in the
history of man. Let no one forget that the people who came
—and still come—to this country are often gifted with that
"extra something" of courage and conviction, that added
belief that all problems in America can be solved.

As President Dwight D. Eisenhower once put it, we
Americans have "a passion for justice." This passion for
justice must now militate to secure the unfinished business
of the Declaration of Independence. It is ironic that Jefferson, who wrote it, held slaves and continued to, while a
Tory governor of Massachusetts, Hutchinson, asked that

if all the truths about equality were so self-evident, then why did they not apply to the blacks? Yet liberty, as Adams pointed out, "implies thought and choice and power," and men were created equal in the sense that they were born to equal rights—"as indubitable as a moral government in the universe." Jefferson himself finally admitted that, "Since God is in the universe, slavery must vanish," but he left more concrete action to later generations.

There is a second society in the world with a drive and dynamism approximately akin to our own, and with purposes wholly different. The Communist world has moved with startling speed away from a unity that once appeared monolithic. Within the Soviet Union, there appears the intellectual ferment and the political unpredictability of a new generation of leaders. The bitter divisions between Soviet and Communist Chinese ideologies and ambitions are reflected in the struggles of Communist factions around the world. Throughout Eastern Europe, the governments and peoples of Romania and Czechoslovakia and others are finding ever bolder ways to assert their views. In Asia, also, the national forms of Communism are evolving in their own ways, and not as the disciplined offshoots of Moscow or Peking.

All this does not make our confrontation with Communism in the world less difficult—but profoundly different. The so-called "just wars of national liberation," as in Vietnam, can be quite as grave a threat as the old-fashioned overt aggression across national frontiers. A divided Communist world can threaten us—and all free peoples—from not one but several centers of hostile power, each of them competing in belligerence. Meanwhile, the Soviet Union's steady increase in its nuclear power is gradually obtaining for the other side a true strategic balance. During the postwar years, we enjoyed an overwhelming nuclear superiority. As late as 1962, we were able to force a Soviet retreat in the Caribbean without having to meet Soviet countermoves, in Berlin or Turkey. But under conditions of growing Soviet strategic power, local crises will become much more dangerous. This is the gravest threat to our national security in the years ahead.

The impact of the Tet offensive in Vietnam upon our national life most closely resembles the earlier effect of Sputnik—and it is here, perhaps, that hope begins. The Soviet success in launching unmanned satellites, swiftly followed by the first man in space, the first rocket to the moon, prompted the most searching re-evaluation of our society since the Depression. This resulted in a great debate about our national purpose, which led in turn to what has since been called our educational explosion. The increase in educational enrollments, the expansion of the high schools and universities, the sharpening of the curricula and the emphasis upon academic accomplishment, have since reached the point that approximately one-half of our young men and women can now expect to obtain a college education.

This, in turn, will inevitably improve the quality of our national life and our message to the rest of the world. And it is plain we can do much better: one out of every three fifth-graders will not finish high school and only one of five high school students *eligible* for college goes on to earn a college *degree*.

The Tet offensive has already limned for all to see the military and political fallacies with which the Vietnam war has been so unproductively waged. Militarily, the Tet offensive stripped the war of its futile, soft and optimistic verbiage about "secure hamlets" and "favorable body counts," as General Giap's forces swept into twenty-six cities almost simultaneously and set them aflame. Ironically, the United States and South Vietnamese forces, called back from the jungle to fight the Communists in the open, won their greatest, bravest and best-led victory of the war.

Politically, the Tet offensive showed that our "pacification" campaign was a failure. We had not given the South Vietnamese the sense of security they needed to succeed in rural development and self-government. We had not been able to help establish a widely based national government in South Vietnam, nor combat the apathy, self-seeking and inexperience that we found there. We had been overly optimistic in seeking to export Western concepts to a land in which political institutions had to be created.

The Tet offensive reminded us above all that the Vietnamese people, as the "controversial" war correspondents on the scene have been trying to tell us for years, are war-weary and worn out. Who can blame them? Their country has been at war since 1941—Japanese, Chinese, warlords, religious sects, Communists of all versions, Frenchmen, Americans and scores of cliques of Vietnamese have ripped

their land asunder for a generation. Surely it is not beyond
our comprehension to imagine how we might feel if our
country had been fought over, for whatever high purpose,
ever since the year of Pearl Harbor.

That having been said—and in other chapters I shall discuss these matters further—I would warn our adversaries
not to "overreact" to our current discomfiture in foreign
relations. In commencing our new quest for honorable
negotiations in Vietnam, we are expressing a sober re-
assessment, not seeking peace at any price. At stake in this
judgment is not only peace in Vietnam but the chances of
peace in Asia, the Middle East and the whole world. Our
adversaries ought not to conclude that we will be unable
to devise an effective strategy against their "wars of national liberation," *i.e.,* subversion, or that other peoples
less weakened than the South Vietnamese will not rise up
against incursion and intrusion.

Specifically, it seems to me that there are three essential
bases for our position in Vietnam peace talks:

1. We will not accept—as we shall not try to impose—
any solution dictated by force.

2. We should accept in South Vietnam's political life
any group that seeks its objectives through the political
process, rather than by pursuing them by force or subversion.

3. We must seek a settlement whose aims and guarantees safeguard the freedom and security of all Southeast
Asia.

Then we can move ahead—in partnership with the free
and prosperous Western European countries, Australia

and Japan—to fight the truly "just wars of national liberation" in Asia—the struggles for political and economic development.

Then too we will be better able to reorder our priorities at home. Our goals must be redefined, and our order of values reassigned. Our objectives must be measured against the means available. We cannot do all things for all men and all communities and all nations at all times. No war can be fought, no slum cleared, no crime curbed, no hospital built, no new worker trained, no teacher paid, "for free." Nor is the arithmetic one of money alone. We must use all of our resources wisely—money, materials and men. And we must plan with an awareness that the act—and the art—of political, economic and humanitarian creation becomes an element of our way of life and our legacy. Only chaos comes quickly. Order takes time. And so in us, as with all pioneers, few virtues will matter more than patience and persistence.

"The peace we seek," as President Eisenhower remarked in his first Inaugural Address, "is nothing less than the fulfillment of our whole faith among ourselves and in our dealings with others. This signifies more than the stilling of guns, easing the sorrow of war. More than an escape from death, it is a way of life. More than a haven for the weary, it is a hope for the brave."

I would add that, first, we must strive to be one thing —and not many things—to all nations and all men, including ourselves. We cannot win the trust and confidence of continents of other colors until we honor our own citizens descended of slaves. We cannot encourage the citizens of

Calcutta, Djakarta, Teheran or Bangkok to defend their freedom and order—not to mention the citizens of Rio de Janeiro, Lima, Panama City and Guatemala City—until we have some meaningful and visible story to tell about how we are cleaning up our slums.

How can we expect to encourage Africa not to discriminate against whites, nor Europe against blacks, if we are unable, or unwilling, or unready to find jobs, education and living standards for our own, all of our own?

Within our own politics, the same rules—the same precepts of integrity—apply with equal force. And if any young man—caring about politics, as he should—were to contemplate a life in politics, and were he to ask my first counsels and warnings, I would tell him these equally plain things: You can only be one thing to all citizens— wherever you go, whatever you say, whatever you seek. You cannot trim your principles to fit your ambitions—or change your convictions as you change your audiences.

Second, we must, as a nation, distrust contentment and shun complacency not only among ourselves but among our leaders. Alexander Hamilton wrote this right into *The Federalist* as an indispensable American trait. "Energy in the executive is a leading character in the definition of good government," he wrote.

Third, we must at least begin to see and to know the horizons of the past and the future. We dare not—we cannot—live as a nation in repose, calmly waiting for each new challenge to emerge on the horizon, advance implacably toward us, and finally confront us in the form of a crisis. We live in an age of revolution and explosion:

exploding bombs, exploding population, revolutionary wars, revolutionary wants. In such an age, we have only two choices, no more. We shall learn to be masters of circumstance—or we shall be its victims.

This, ultimately, is why the common sense and the dignity of our political life, and the clarity and conviction of our political purposes, will write the future of our nation —for it is through our politics that we give speech and life to the values of freedom we seek to guard. Let us state plainly the full truth of the matter: We do not seek merely to guard these values for our own national safety, but also because we know that only with the saving of these values can America inhabit a world where freedom and justice and law and peace can also live.

Our national task—the task of all of us, in our daily lives—is not merely to demonstrate that the truths and practices of our country are right. We need also to prove, by our exertions and our example, that these values are relevant—relevant to all the peoples of the world and their unfolding destinies.

Let no one dismiss this as mere aspiration or as simply an admirable but abstract need of the spirit. The need of which I speak is, in fact, a most practical need. We need a sense of full purpose—a dream, if you will. We need such a dream in order to live the waking life in this troubled world. For without such a sense of purpose—such a dream —we could only be a nation of sleepwalkers, stumbling toward an ever deeper darkness.

— II —

THE MIDDLE
OF THE ROAD

At 9:25 P.M., Eastern Standard Time, Sunday, March 31, 1968, President Lyndon B. Johnson fortified his televised proposals for Vietnam peace talks with a startling announcement: "I will not seek, nor will I accept, the nomination of my party as your President." I respect and commend the President's initiative in exploring the possibilities of an honorable settlement with North Vietnam. His courageous spirit of self-sacrifice was a significant contribution to the ending of our own, increasingly malignant controversy between "hawks" and "doves," and a long step toward the restoration of national unity.

But where will our next leadership come from—and in

what mood, and from what direction will it measure our problems and attempt to deal with them? Irrespective of personalities, will the new leadership come from the left, the right, or the center? Will the nominees of the parties reflect the polarization of our people—or the need for unity?

The basic thrust of my own decision to become an active candidate for the Presidency was to provide a choice within the Republican Party. I have a feeling that ideology is not as big a factor now as the desire on the part of the party and the country to find unity and to find constructive action to meet the problems. I think there is more pragmatism, if you like, in the feeling of the people than before. I think we recognize we cannot afford the luxury of ideological debates which are unrelated to the problems we face—problems which have tremendous reality and are of deep concern to us all.

I have an even deeper concern that the American people are, in a way, losing confidence in themselves and in our institutions. I do not feel this is justified. I understand that the speed of change is a source of great frustration— and with frustration comes uncertainty—and with uncertainty comes fear. Sometimes the problems seem insoluble —but I do not think they are insoluble. I think that with a better understanding of the problems, they can be dealt with.

I think we have no reason to lose faith in ourselves or our institutions. This has been the great strength of America in the past—the confidence of the people, our belief in ourselves, and our belief that we can and will solve the problems before us. I feel this is just as true today, and just as valid, and that, together, we can reach our goals.

One of the problems has been that we have not fully understood the meaning of change, the dimensions of change, or the impact of what is taking place. Therefore our actions have become less relevant to the needs of our time. And so we have become less effective in our leadership. I think we need to get back to a better understanding of problems of change. I think we need to shape change to serve our purposes instead of letting it overwhelm us in the form of crises, which is what has been happening.

In times like these, especially, the irrelevance of the ideologist and the extremist to solution of the problems we face becomes increasingly clear.

The middle of the road may sound flat and unglamorous to some. Yet it can mean courage, faith and excitement in the worth and dignity of free men. It can mean understanding of our basic rights of equal opportunity and our cherished, federal system of shared sovereignty, checks and balances, and nobody able to run anybody else in a tyrannous sense for very long.

The middle of the road suggests teamwork and partnership—and this, of course, is what we need more than anything else right now. Somehow we are going to have to find ways of enlisting all the volunteer talents and resources of our great nation to cope with the problems before us. This means the mobilization not only of national, state and local government; it also means the

channeling of investment capital, modern science, techno-
logical skills, business acumen, labor statesmanship, educational ventures and intellectual daring. The critical fact
is that the potential outside government—the potential
to power economic and social growth, provide jobs and
more jobs, raise capital, manage it prudently, assemble resources, organize—is many times greater than anything
that government can accomplish on its own.

The middle of the road, most importantly, offers us
all the opportunity to participate. The existence of the
nation, it might be argued, has no real significance from
the standpoint of humanity at large unless it means the
participation of the people—unless this truly is, in fact,
government of, by, and for the people.

How can American citizens polarize into frowning, hostile monoliths of right and left? Normally, we must be
content if each of us can do something—not all that we
wish, but something—for the advancement of those principles of righteousness which underlie true national greatness. It has been said that our success in accomplishing
anything depends very much upon our not trying to accomplish everything. Yet we *must* advance step by step
toward our goals. We know there are many injustices
which we, as individuals, are powerless to remedy. But we
know also that there is much injustice—instances in our
individual lives, happening every day—which can be
remedied. There are certain steps in our lives that can
be taken. The important thing is generally "the next
step"—and, in the middle of the road, we can safely join

with others who wish to take it, and walk together, and work together, without fretting overmuch about any theories they may have about, say, the two-hundredth step, which is not in sight.

No one of us can make the world move on very far. But it moves at all only when each one of a very large number undertakes, soberly and sensibly, to do the possible. So if anyone goes into a meeting with his fellow citizens, and tries to analyze a problem, and work out how it can be solved, with armbands that say "I am looking for a liberal solution," or "I am looking for a conservative solution," all he is doing is blinding himself to the realities. It is something like saying: "My mind is made up! Don't confuse me with the facts!"

Such labels are misleading, and out of date, in the context of the massive problems that we face. Rather, I would say that, today, we must be conservative in our loyalty to eternal truths that define the nature, the freedom, the dignity of man. We must be liberal in our constant and tireless quest to find ever new ways to meet ever new threats to this freedom and dignity. And we must also be progressive in a spirit that rejects escape to yesterdays that, perhaps, never existed—while looking ahead with optimism and confidence to the tomorrows of ever more secure liberty, more universal justice, more fruitful peace. This is the middle-course pathway of our journey to national unity—and how desperately we need to take it, today.

Then we will not have to worry: "Are we doing something which is conservative?" "Are we being too liberal?" Then we will be searching and working together for the right answers.

Why, then, as a would-be unifier of this Nation, am I a Republican, and why am I seeking the Republican nomination for the Presidency? This is a fair question. I have, in fact, important philosophical differences with the recent conduct of our affairs at the federal level—in terms of the basic principles on which the nation has been built.

I do not believe that the two most recent Administrations have shown a clear understanding of our free enterprise system. I do not believe that the role of government in this regard has been adequately appreciated. That role should be to create a framework of laws, administrative actions, and attitudes which will remove the harassments and hurdles to the effective functioning of a fair and growing free enterprise system, which will expand the incentives for a more rapid rate of economic growth to produce the increased job opportunities and higher living standards the people are seeking.

I do not believe that these Administrations have shown sufficient understanding of sound financial management in government. They have not understood the vital factor of confidence, so essential to our national economic expansion, our international financial standing, our balance of payments, our defense of the dollar.

I do not believe that these Administrations have valued adequately the functioning of a truly federal system— the shared sovereignty concept of the Founding Fathers.

They have failed to mobilize the creative energies of state and local government. On the contrary, they have attempted to make the system work by expanding constantly the reach of the federal executive branch, producing tension and resistance from the other branches, and by moving the nation toward a greater and greater centralization of real power in Washington.

I do not believe that these Administrations have shown their understanding that alliances are exactly that—alliances—for time and again they have ridden roughshod over the interests, hopes and doubts of our closest friends. It is characteristic that even our peace overtures to North Vietnam were launched in a manner to stir concern among our friends in Southeast Asia who now feel themselves directly menaced.

In the critical field of individual liberties, one can find a pattern of government misunderstanding of our checks and balances and limited powers.

There is, in fact, an almost unlimited arsenal of weapons available in the government for tolerable or intolerable use against business—powers which might easily be abused. These include: antitrust suits; federal licensing and regulation of food, drugs, power sites, communications and airlines, among others; federal subsidies and rates; the award—and tentative award—of federal research, development, construction and purchase contracts, and the withholding of them; and, in the hands of arbitrary men, the possibility of special Internal Revenue investigations of corporate personnel of all levels.

There is also a virtually unlimited arsenal for use—

and abuse—against labor, although this is more subtly deployed. By raising questions about a labor leader's personal affairs, by indicating that he is about to be investigated by the FBI or other agencies, by instituting and prolonging such on-again, off-again intimidation, the federal government is able to undermine his prestige with his own rank and file. This is aside from the powers and influences available through the federal agencies directly concerned with labor problems.

But the implications of this government power—to strangle business and labor—run deeper. The placement or cancellation of government contracts can mean economic life or death for whole communities and whole populations. It does not take much imagination for us to realize that tyranny, in our country, might, narrowly, conceivably, be possible, if only for a limited period before our national wisdom and strength reasserted themselves.

Much must depend upon the principles motivating the actions of those who wield the great authority vested in the federal government and its departments and agencies.

The great power that the people of this nation have given to the federal government—and have not taken away —was given on the express premise that it will be used for the development of a more perfect union, for justice, for domestic tranquillity, for the common defense, for the general welfare and to secure the blessings of liberty for ourselves and posterity.

The use of the vast arsenal of federal political power must, therefore, be for these great objectives, if it is to be legitimate. The purpose of holding office and exercising authority is to seek and to achieve these specific goals in accordance with the basic principles of liberty and human dignity.

Power is, therefore, not to be sought for the sake of power itself. The pursuit of principle must not be subverted to opportunism, to a preoccupation with the privileges of office, to any impulse of assuaging one's own insecurity by pushing others around.

Personally, as well as politically, I am extremely sensitive on questions of individual liberties because I have seen the purveyors of hate and distrust in action. They have no solutions for the problems of unemployment, of education, of retraining, housing, and racial injustice. Their attitude to the rest of the world is simply: go away. It is in terms of my emphasis on individual liberties that I would work for national unity today.

The government needs also to define a reasonable attitude toward protest and dissent. One might think that this is becoming the most popular sport on our campuses and elsewhere. It is, of course, much more. It is a serious sign of our times—times of swift change—challenges to old institutions—revolts of new ideas. And let me state first of all one basic fact: The spirit of protest and dissent—and the energetic advocacy of change—are true and vital elements of our tradition of freedom. I would therefore enter my own sharp dissent, for example, from those who would sweepingly dismiss and denounce the turbulence in 1968 at New York's Columbia University as a sign of nothing less than a "revolutionary struggle to seize the universities of this country." Such a mass indictment is unjust and unrealistic. The provost of Columbia himself deplored such a condemnation as "a dramatic oversimplification." And this kind of oversimplification clouds rather than clarifies the true issue. There are, in fact, two basic issues involved:

The first is: we must recognize the healthy purposes of protest.

And the second is: we must respect the proper methods and limits of protest.

To suggest these proper limits, I would again cite some wise words from several professors of the Columbia Law School in a "Declaration of Confidence" in that university's future. They warned that "the force of reason" must be the strength of protest, and not "the force of massed bodies." And they further said: "Using muscles instead of minds has no place in the academic setting." I share that principle and I echo that warning. For it is an essential truth that there are certain basic human rights that any protest must not injure or defy. These include: the right *not* to be threatened by force of violence, the right to privacy, the right to free movement, the right to free access to public buildings, the right to be appealed to by *argument* rather than by threat. It is true of the life of a university, as it is true of a democracy, that the avenue of change must be persuasion, not coercion.

The first task of a dissident minority must therefore be to enlist and even arouse the majority—not defy it. The thrust of this kind of protest is positive. It is not enough simply to denounce, to tear down, to walk out, or even to sit in. A real change in our institutions—whenever such change is needed—will not come from this kind of negativism. It will come from the action of builders—not from men and women attempting to wreck the old, but from those who would replace it with something better.

In this context, there is also a new need in government to listen much more carefully to older people and to pay more attention to their aspirations. There is something of a preoccupation with youth in this country, as young people themselves concede, and there is a rising sentiment that once an American is no longer young, he or she does not count. The emphasis on Medicare, on welfare for the aging, the phrase "senior citizen" itself, is symptomatic of a tendency to put older people "out to grass." The danger in the formation of a *cult* of youth in national affairs is that our country might act impulsively and immaturely, thoughtlessly and overambitiously, heading in all directions at once.

On the other hand, I would say it is up to older people to deliver judgments and actions that may be recognized as wise and effective. C. P. Snow once attended one of our New York State conventions on the aging, and he pointed out a simple and startling fact to us. It was an extremely rare thing in the pre-industrial world, said Lord Snow, to see one's grandchildren. It was rare for the fairly convincing reason that one was not likely to live that long. In our time, we have extended life to the point that to know one's great-grandchildren is scarcely unusual, but if we only add years to our lives, then we are merely aging. If, however, we continue to increase our education and our experience and our contribution to society, then we are maturing in a helpful way.

We need to establish, in our view of ourselves, that older people are just as different from one another as youth from youth—and this awareness of individuality is what touches the spirits of men and women, and adds meaning to the quality of life. We need to remember, while we ponder the reasons for the rebelliousness of youth, that it is infinitely more heartbreaking that so many of our old people are lonely, neglected, even rejected, their feeling of usefulness all too often an aching need. Why should a busy bank president head a community fund drive when a retired bank president can do as good a job? Why should a distracted mother try to spend two afternoons a week at volunteer work in a hospital if a healthy retired businesswoman can do the job as well, and wants to?

In this rising opportunity for older, as well as young, people to play a part in our national life lies one of the hidden, human challenges for our country in the 1970's and 1980's. And, as I must emphasize, citizen participation flourishes most hopefully in the middle of the road of our society.

The Republican Party has also always known its best times in the middle of the road. It is a party which has met the emerging needs of our nation since the Emancipation. Its accomplishments include: The abolition of slavery. The preservation of the Union. The purchase of Alaska. The Homestead Act. The long frontier and the settlement of the West. The Civil Service. The Sherman Anti-Trust Act. The alliance with Great Britain and Canada. The first hemisphere conferences. The first national conservation programs. The Pure Food and Drug Act. The creation of the Department of Labor and Department of Commerce. The Panama Canal. The Great White Fleet. The Court of International Justice. The Health, Education and Welfare Department. The federal interstate highway system. Open Skies—and the beginning of arms control. Peace in Korea. Deterrence of Communism. The National Defense Education Act.

There is much more to the achievement of such progress than pragmatism, of course, but partnership in problem solving within the framework of our great federal idea is what we need most in America right now.

Let me first make it clear that I do not speak of the federal idea as merely a mechanical, technical, or abstract formula for government operations. I refer to the federal idea, broadly, as a concept of government by which a sovereign people, for their greater progress and protection, yield a portion of their sovereignty to a political system that has more than one center of sovereign power, energy and creativity. No one of these centers or levels has the power to destroy another. Under the Constitution, for example, there are two principal centers of government power, federal and state. As a practical matter, local government, by delegation of state authority under the principle of "home rule," is a third such key center of power. The federal idea, then, is above all an idea of shared sovereignty—at all times responsive to the needs and the will of the people in whom sovereignty ultimately resides.

Our federal idea is complex and subtle. It involves a balance of strengths. It puts into play a sharing of powers not only among different levels of government but—on each level—a separation of powers between the legislative, executive, and judicial branches of the government. And it clearly signifies more than mere governmental structure. It demands faith in—and an environment for—the free play of individual initiative in terms of business, labor, farmers, political parties, universities, science, social associations, community groups and all the other elements of what Madison, long ago, predicted to be "the multiplicity of interest." All these must operate, in the terms of the federal idea, within a framework of laws and principles affirming dignity and freedom.

A federal system, then, seeks stability without rigidity, security without inertia, flexibility without drift. It encourages innovation and inventiveness, governed by principle and guided by purpose. It assures responsiveness more thoughtful than mere reflex—and liberty that does not lapse toward anarchy. In short, it seeks to hold the delicately precarious balance between freedom and order upon which depend, decisively, the freedom, peace and prosperity of all of us.

"Despite its extreme American accent," Russell Davenport wrote, "what is it but a way of observing the universal truth, best stated by a nineteenth-century English liberal on the subject of India, that 'self-government is better than good government.'" People should do as much as possible for themselves, and by themselves, at all levels of society, and there is a presumption against any government, state or national, that proclaims a new need for its intervention. Jefferson said that, "If we can prevent the government from wasting the labors of the people under pretense of taking care of them, they must become happy." And in the words of that great philosopher, Jimmy Durante, "Don't put no constrictions on da people. Leave 'em ta hell alone."

Today, the federal idea is in fact the middle of the road. "It is derided by all of the right and the left," says President Eisenhower. "They deliberately misrepresent the central position as a neutral, wishy-washy one. Yet here is the truly creative area within which we may obtain agreement for constructive social action compatible with basic American principles—and with the just aspirations of every sincere American. It is the area in which are rooted the hopes and allegiances of the vast majority of the people."

III

PROBLEM

SOLVING

IN THE CITIES

If it be thy design to ornament the City by thy gifts, be thou thyself dedicated, in the first place, to whatsoever is loveliest; and of Clemency, Justice and Benevolence, thou shalt raise aloft the best and most memorable monument within the Republic, not merely an inconsiderable building. For, if Reason should rule in cities, it is better certainly for great souls to inhabit small houses than for men slaves to lurk in magnificent mansions.
—Epictetus

JOBLESS RATE DROPS EXCEPT IN SLUMS
—New York *Daily News*

It was twenty minutes to midnight on a rainy Sunday evening. The Illinois Central's *City of New Orleans* pulled into its main Chicago station at Michigan Avenue and the lakefront. A young Negro stirred himself and peered through the rain-specked window at his new home. He was in Chicago—a long haul from the shack he had left at the edge of a Tennessee cotton hamlet. He had left the

South on a wandering search for work and for a better life
and he expected to find this in the Northern cities.

As the train jolted to a stop, the young man got up and
took down a metal suitcase, tied with string to keep it
shut, from the rack overhead. He smiled at the thin, shy
woman behind him who was struggling with an armload
of children, cardboard boxes and shopping bags. Then he
walked quickly out of the train, past the Travelers Aid
station, toward the stairway to the street. "Don't talk to
nobody," a friend had warned him. "Keep away from the
colored cab drivers outside the station. They'll charge you
five dollars just to get to Lawndale."

The young Negro paused under a street light and took a
crumpled piece of paper from his shirt pocket. On it was
written the address of a cousin, and the sentence: "Take
the No. 12 bus out Roosevelt Road. . . ." And he set out
to find the No. 12 bus—another anonymous arrival in the
vast migration of rural, undereducated, unskilled Negroes
and whites to the cold, crowded, terrifying and yet not
wholly hopeless cities of the industrial states.

In 1910, 91 percent of America's 9.8 million Negroes
lived in the South—and only 27 percent in cities of 2,500
population or more. Between 1910 and 1966, the total
Negro population more than doubled, to 21.5 million, and
the number of Negroes living in metropolitan areas rose
from 2.6 million to 14.8 million. The population of Negroes
outside the South increased elevenfold from 880,000 to 9.7
million. As far as it can be determined, between 1940 and
1963, approximately 3,300,000 Negroes left the South. Be-

tween 1960 and 1966 more than 600,000 Negro migrants arrived from the South in Northern and Western cities. The young Negro beginning his new life at the Illinois Central station in Chicago in the middle of the night could expect to live in a slum. Between 16 and 20 percent of Negroes in the cities live in squalor and deprivation as measured by governmental health, education and sanitation statistics. He would have a difficult time finding satisfactory employment: the Labor Department recently reported that the national unemployment rate was down to 3.5 percent, but that unemployment among slum dwellers was 7 percent, and among Negro slum dwellers 8.7 per cent. The Bureau of Labor Statistics Commissioner, Arthur M. Ross, commented that the unemployment rate for Negroes everywhere was 6.7 percent as compared to 3.1 percent for whites everywhere and, "although Negroes have made some employment gains, it is a matter of running pretty fast to stand still." Then there is a category known as "sub-employment": this means unemployment and partial, part-time, haphazard, odd-job employment. The sub-employment rate of Negroes in the slums is about 33 percent—more than eight times greater than the national unemployment level.

I am zeroing in on the situation confronting this young Negro beginning his new life because this gets to the heart of the agony of our cities today. It also contributes mightily and perhaps decisively to the racial crisis within the cities crisis. The Social Security Administration defines the poverty level in our country at an income of $3,335 per

year for a nonfarm family of four. More than 40 percent
of Negroes below this poverty level dwell in the slums—
and they are caught in an appalling trap of bad health,
rats, garbage, exploitation, prostitution, dope addiction,
insecurity and crime. The crime rates in one Negro slum,
for example, are running more than thirty-five times higher
than the crime rates in an average high-income white district. Thirty-five times! Needless to say, this dreadful situation leads to riots and civil disorders that sometimes appear
to be setting our whole country on fire.

The President's National Advisory Commission on Civil
Disorders—very closely heeded by most of our people—is
quite specific on this point, and it has amassed more than
600 pages of objective evidence to buttress its conclusions.
The Commission identified twelve deeply held grievances
that led to the riots of 1967, and ranked these into three
levels of relative intensity. These were, according to the
Commission:

First Level of Intensity
1. Police practices.
2. Unemployment and underemployment.
3. Inadequate housing.

Second Level of Intensity
4. Inadequate education.
5. Poor recreation facilities and programs.
6. Ineffectiveness of the political structure and grievance
   mechanisms.

Third Level of Intensity
7. Disrespectful white attitudes.
8. Discriminatory administration of justice.

9. Inadequacy of federal programs.
10. Discriminatory consumer and credit practices.
11. Inadequate welfare programs.

Assuming, as we must, that the Negro resentment of the police reflects their resentment against the white "Establishment," and also assuming, as we must, that police brutality can be and will always be curbed, then we are left with a very important conclusion. In my opinion, the riots of 1967 were not caused by widespread racial hatred and incompatibility, as the extremists on both sides of the crisis would have us believe. There is an ample area of goodwill. There is a fantastic opportunity here for the problem solvers. And the key targets are, to repeat:

UNEMPLOYMENT AND UNDEREMPLOYMENT
INADEQUATE HOUSING

Whitney M. Young, Jr., the brilliant, thoughtful executive director of the National Urban League, zeroes in more closely. He says: "The core of the civil rights problem is the matter of achieving equal opportunity for Negroes in the labor market. For it stands to reason that all our other civil rights depend on that one for fulfillment. We cannot afford better education for our children, better housing or medical care unless we have jobs. The present situation is a disaster for our country."

I ask—and I shall try to answer—the question of how to meet the test. Let me promptly state three ways in which we cannot do so.

First, we cannot meet it with traditional concepts and conventional programs. We cannot respond merely with endless exhorting, or endless federal deficit financing. Nor can we meet it by pitting the need for order against the need for progress. For without progress—and without justice—there will be no order.

Second, we cannot fight our way through this trial with the arsenal of violence and revenge. For the oppressed and the outraged, as well as the oppressors and outragers, these are weapons of self-destruction. The fires that should be lighted are not in stores and warehouses. They must be in the hearts of our citizens and the halls of our government.

Third, we cannot meet this test with promises and programs conceived narrowly or separately for the black community or the white community. The conditions of black citizens and white citizens do vary, but their deepest aspirations do not. And the cry of the Negro is not simply a claim on the national economy: it is a sweeping quest for personal dignity. Such dignity means the respected and self-respecting right to live and learn, work and vote, prosper and hope, as freely and fully as any free men on earth.

It is the whole American community, white and black, that now must make its resolve clear and firm. For long—for decades—a large and complacent part of this community has sought to hide, as it were, behind the sign "Do Not Disturb." For them, the American dream became the American slumber. But now the individual citizen—especially the more favored and fortunate—simply must care enough to give of himself. He must care enough to shed bias, to deny self, and to live with respect and honor for the dignity of his neighbor. And he must give enough to respond to the kind of national leadership that asks more than it promises.

A resolute national leadership must sharply define our goals and clearly assign their order of values, and must rigorously assess the means available. The genius of our federal idea is that we will be able to move to meet the problems, to solve the problems, with flexibility, urgency, and, above all, with a true sense of partnership at the problem-solving level.

I have spent the greater part of my life in problem solving of this nature. Obviously, I believe that government has a very high responsibility and role of a positive character to play in our country. But I would not dream of suggesting, in wildest fancy, that government can do it alone—for I have a similar faith in and commitment to the private enterprise system. How to mobilize the leadership, the inventiveness, the know-how, the goodwill that helped build and sustain our way of life and our productive meaning for mankind. How to deploy these mighty forces most effectively, against the other America's poverty, unemployment, ill health, undereducation, violence and despair. I would not delude myself that private enterprise can accomplish the task on its own, either. Let us look for guidance by glancing back, briefly, across our recent history:

There was the post-Civil War period, when the problem for the Republican Party was to create and fashion a durable framework for our change from an agricultural to an industrial society, while at the same time we became more engaged in world affairs.

There was the Great Depression, when it fell to the Democratic Party to accept and honor the government's responsibility to fight perils and ills beyond the individual's power of self-defense. And the nation, once again, grew stronger through its travail and better for its trial.

I think now we are in a third new period. The size and the sweep of the challenges have changed again—and today the challenge is to create the mechanism, to provide the incentive and the administrative plans of action, which will encourage a full participation by the private powers of our society—social and economic, business, labor, finance, research and development, the universities, everybody—so that we can help solve the problems of the poor people of this country, each of us playing our rightful part.

In the new context of our federal idea, the place of national government itself becomes new. It must become not the great monolith—but the great catalyst. It must inspire rather than impose. And it must find its highest concern to be not supervision, but vision. I believe deeply in such a new government, such a new leadership and such a new America. I believe the whole American commonwealth can give no less.

Hopefully, there are signs of a broadening national consensus on the new need for partnership in change. Business is increasingly aware of its opportunity to become the engine of progress in such areas as civil rights, poverty, urban decay and pollution of the environment. Businessmen are increasingly aware of the need to demonstrate, through action, that the profit motive, properly employed, constitutes a powerful tool with which to achieve our national goals. Former Secretary of Commerce Alexander Trowbridge estimates that, to bring down the level of Negro unemployment to that of white unemployment, business would have to find or make 350,000 new jobs for Negroes, and annually this would add more than $1 billion annually to the national output and subtract millions from public welfare costs. Whitney Young says also that "big business . . . is becoming more enlightened and is beginning to see the need as well as the ultimate potential of adding Negroes to its staff and production forces." As for "big labor," Whitney Young adds that labor unions are more concerned than ever before with the problem of rooting out discrimination, and he hailed as a "breakthrough" the finding by our New York State Commission for Human Rights that Local 28 of the Sheet Metal Workers in New York had discriminated historically against Negroes. If discrimination within unions can be proven to exist, he said, "and if this principle can be moved into National Labor Relations Board activities, it will provide a strong, though admittedly limited, new weapon against bias in unions."

The newly formed Urban Coalition, consisting of more than 1,200 business, labor, religious, civil rights, government and other leaders, proclaims the need for "programs instead of promises." *Fortune* magazine confirms that dozens of aggressive corporate programs are under way for hiring, training and promoting more Negroes—"and many companies with ambitious programs, not wanting to seem to promise anything they cannot deliver, are wisely refusing to discuss them yet." A few examples of business initiative—and I am sure there are many others of which I am not aware—might include:

• Avco Corporation, with a federal training grant of $1,148,000 and its own direct investment of $2,300,000, is establishing a project to employ between 200 and 250 hard-core unemployables in the Roxbury section of Boston.

• Aerojet-General Corporation, a West Coast subsidiary of General Tire and Rubber, invested $1,300,000 in setting up the Watts Manufacturing Company to conduct simple manufacturing operations in the hard-pressed riot area of Los Angeles. It won a government contract for $2,500,000 worth of tents and now has a backlog of another $2,500,000 of orders for tents, metal parts and wooden shipping crates, and expects to increase its employment to 900 men and women.

• Lockheed Aircraft Corporation, with its huge defense contracts, has long been a pioneer in hiring and promoting Negroes, and is now experimenting with retraining and employing hard-core unemployables for its aerospace plants in Sunnyvale, Calif., and Marietta, Ga., 75 percent Negroes, and 25 percent with police records. At Marietta, candidates for the Lockheed program are recruited with the help of the National Urban League, the National Association for the Advancement of Colored People, and others. Sixty-five out of the first ninety candidates "graduated" and three have since been promoted, one of them twice—a record that has led the company to train 200 more at Marietta alone this year. Lockheed's corporate personnel director, Eugene G. Mattison, says: "Motivation is the key. These people simply don't believe what you tell them. They think what you're offering is just another chance to fail. You have to persuade them that notwithstanding any disappointments they've had, there's really something for them now if they prepare themselves, apply themselves, and work."

· General Motors Corporation, working with the Urban League, hired several hundred unemployables and agreed to refrain, for a period, from dismissing them for tardiness, absence, or lack of ability. If a worker failed to show up for work, a member of a "follow-up committee" might go to the man's home, haul him out of bed and bring him to the plant, or take some other appropriate action. General Motors says that 73 percent of the "unemployables" are still on the job, and that others will soon be taken on at other plants.

· The Ford Motor Company hired 3,400 hard-core unemployed in Detroit after the riots and expects to take on a total of 4,000 to 6,000 "unemployables." "We screened them in, not out," said a Ford official. Ford for a while hired all applicants for jobs at its two hiring stations in the slums unless they were narcotics addicts or habitual criminals, so long as they were literate enough to fill out an application form and could pass a physical examination.

There are, in fact, countless programs, largely of an inchoate nature, springing up all over the country, often founded on spontaneous moves by businessmen, local government and interested citizens. One of the more elaborate of these is the National Alliance of Businessmen, which is attempting to find 18,500 permanent jobs for impoverished adults by June 1969 and 35,700 summer jobs for underprivileged youths. This Alliance simply sends young executives, on their company time, to potential employers of the unemployable to ask for their help. One young credit analyst with Manufacturers Hanover Trust in New York City called on more than thirty firms, and got a few pledges of jobs, before meeting the manager of a dye works in the Bronx, who told him: "I'll call a meeting of all the dyers and wholesale dry cleaners in my area who'll come. Most of them have job openings. Maybe we can set up a joint training program and do ourselves and the Alliance a favor. We ought to come up with better than fifty jobs." Floyd D. Hall, chairman of the board of Eastern Air Lines and the New York City director of the National Alliance of Businessmen, warns: "Let us not forget the consequences of any failure to act in this emergency. Let us not forget that many of our sometimes noisy but relatively comfortable commuter trains pass through these parts of New York City that are most likely to erupt if action is not taken."

Thomas J. Watson, Jr., chairman of the board of International Business Machines, recently announced that IBM would lease an old warehouse in a slum section of New York City and convert it into a plant employing 300 local residents. "A slum is normally the last place you would want to invest in," he said, but he added: "A very large company has a responsibility to society as well as to its employees and stockholders."

The problems are infinitely greater than this hopeful survey of the new trends might indicate. *The New York Times* pointed out, in its story about the IBM decision, that "investing in a rundown area presents enormous risks. The community usually contains a large percentage of high school dropouts, so workmen often require more costly training. Usable real estate is hard to find, and more expensive than suburban acreage, when it can be located. Vandalism means continual security problems and employees from outside the community are often afraid to work there. Local groups, imbued with the growing idea that they should control their own communities, demand roles in business decision-making that executives are extremely reluctant to grant." And when a leading consultant on business locations asked 700 companies if they would be interested in investing in slum areas, 112 said they might be, but not under current conditions. The others were not interested at all, and the 112 laid down all kinds of terms ranging from the elimination of deteriorated buildings to a "guarantee" of responsible local leadership.

"In other words," said the *Times,* "make Harlem like Princeton, N.J., and we'd be delighted to move in. . . . It would take an enormous public subsidy to make private investment feasible, tax credits for new plants, job training and retraining programs, interest rate subsidies, rent supplements. Business is just not ready to help the poor on its own."

Nor is it able—on its own. Business needs partnership just as much as government—and both need the support of the public. This means not only a positive, approving response for the partnership against poverty, but a readiness to accept higher taxes where genuinely needed, whether at federal, state or local levels. These tax increases need not be as high as we might fear if our economic growth, as I shall show in a subsequent chapter on government finance, is sustained and powered upward. In any event, the alternatives are inflation—by endless federal deficit spending—or inaction, letting the problems simply lie there to grow. Inaction will inevitably cost the country in riot damage alone more than any foreseeable tax increase—not to mention loss of life—not to mention our community structure—not to mention our meaning to the rest of the world as a law-abiding nation that is conscious of human rights and dignity.

I therefore recommend action in a phased, practical attack upon the multiple problems of the city. First, there should be an immediate increase of $10 billion a year in federal aid to the states and the cities to meet the immediate problems and needs of our metropolitan areas. This represents about one year's growth factor of federal revenues. In New York, the federal government collects 68 percent of all taxes paid by our citizens, and the state collects 14 percent. Local governments collect the remaining 18 percent. We are struggling to do the best we can with that 14 percent, but our problems grow and grow. We are for example the recipients of this tremendous migration which I described at the beginning of this chapter. I vetoed a one-year residency requirement for welfare not long ago because my conviction is that we are all citizens of one country—and if we get to the point that we are building little residency requirement walls around one another, to protect ourselves from the free movement of men, money and goods, then we are beginning to abridge the meaning of our Federal Union and our Constitution. Nevertheless, we do need help.

To match this federal increase of $10 billion per year, I recommend that the state and local governments across the country increase their own revenues—by growth or taxation—by $10 billion per year. With this increase in the availability of funds for the problems of the urban regions, I believe we will be able to meet many of the problems of education, health, manpower retraining, summer jobs, day-care centers for the children of working mothers, and so on. This is where government as an institution might well play its most useful role.

I would add in this category that, since the cities are already taxing close to their practical limits, the states will have to accept the greater role in the mustering of new resources. This being so, the states should insist on greater responsibility for channeling the funds than has been the case. Federal aid now comes in some 400 aid programs. In the future, federal aid should be provided through a combination of special grants for special purposes, bloc grants and unrestricted per capita aid grants directly to the states and the cities. This means the exercise on the part of the national government of an investment of faith—in the spirit of the federal idea—in the freedom and responsibility of state and city governments to handle the problems closest to their people.

Then there will be the future building of the city—and here private enterprise figures much more importantly. I recommend that there be spent for capital improvements —housing, urban development, industrial expansion and relocation, transportation—a total of $15 billion per year. This is of course a tremendous sum. It can only be raised, and intelligently managed, with the full involvement and enthusiasm of private enterprise. And that means the provision of real incentives for business to invest in poverty areas. The obvious method in which this can be done is the provision of tax incentives for the corporations that take the risks. Then the national and state governments must apply the key lesson to be read in the growth of our economy. This is the imaginative and responsible use of credit. Precisely such use of credit has been pioneered during this decade in New York State, where we have met and dealt with problems typical of the whole country.

Under creative federal leadership, these methods can be applied across the nation in three distinct ways:

First, for the construction of facilities that are not self-supporting, such as schools and parks and mass transport, the states and localities should authorize "full faith and credit" bonds, with some form of federal support if and when necessary. A total of at least $30 billion of such financing will be needed nationally over the next ten years, in my opinion.

Second, there are public projects for which the physical facilities can be made self-supporting. These include universities, hospitals, and middle-income housing. For these, the states and localities, again with federal support if and when necessary, should create credit agencies and authorities to issue self-liquidating revenue bonds, investing some $60 billion over ten years.

Third, incentives to attract private capital for the rebuilding of slum areas must be provided. This can be accomplished on a large scale all over the country by agencies such as New York State's wholly new Urban Development Corporation.

With an authorization to issue $1 billion of self-liquidating bonds, this Urban Development Corporation can attract as much as $5 billion in private capital. If the concept spreads, this could well involve a commitment of private capital to urban development corporations everywhere of as much as $60 billion, or more, to mount a really massive attempt to eradicate the American slum.

If I am told, as I sometimes am, that this aggregate estimate of a public and private capital investment of $150 billion in the next decade is "pie in the sky," I would reply that it most certainly is not because every program recommended is in action in the State of New York.

The alternatives are deficit spending and inaction. Deficit spending can lead to inflation. And inflation hits the farmers—the costs of equipment, fertilizer, fungicides, pesticides, herbicides, increase at a rate higher than the prices the farmers may expect to obtain for their products. Inflation hits the workingmen in the factories—their increases in earnings are eaten up by the same higher prices and the increases in the cost of living. Inflation most cruelly hits the men and women on fixed incomes and all of the poor. The housewife—I do not have to elaborate.

The other alternative is inaction. And the final, searching question is this: Do my countrymen really want to solve the problems of our cities—or not? Measuring the mass of the problem, and its malignancy, I must conclude that this alternative would be unacceptable. As the point of the parable of the Good Samaritan put the alternative:

The others in the parable just passed by.
They did not injure the man.
They just passed by.

We cannot pass by this problem if America is to have a decent future.

IV

CRIME &
REHABILITATION

Not long ago, I held a series of "town meetings" that brought me into every section of New York State. These are informal affairs in which any citizen may ask his Governor any question he chooses—and I find them invaluable as a barometer of public concern. One item very much on my questioners' minds was the high incidence of crime—and it is also very much on mine.

The FBI says that all kinds of crimes have increased by 88 percent since 1960—the population increased by 9 percent—and that all kinds of serious crimes have increased by 62 percent.

The FBI also says that during the first nine months of 1967, the national crime rate escalated as follows:

- All forms of crime, up 16 percent.
- Forcible rape, up 7 percent.
- Aggravated assault, up 9 percent.
- Murder, up 16 percent.
- Robberies, up 27 percent.
- Narcotics arrests, up 28 percent over the whole year.

Crime in the big cities increased by 10 percent—a fact that underscores my point that poverty is the father of crime. But the highest rate of increase in the incidence of crime—13 percent—occurred in our more affluent suburbs. Crime is a problem interlinked with the crisis of the city but it exists of its own nature. What is wrong when youngsters between the ages of ten and seventeen, whites and Negroes, commit one-third of the major crimes in this country, specifically including 20 percent of all robberies, 41 percent of all burglaries and, perhaps not so surprisingly, 52 percent of auto thefts? It is not demagogic to point out that we may have the highest standard of living in the world, but we dare not stroll through our parks at night, dare not send our children to neighborhood playgrounds without apprehension or anxiety, dare not turn down a panhandler too abruptly at night without running the risk of insult or common assault. The President's Commission on Law Enforcement and the Administration of Justice recently reported that 15 percent of all Americans wished to change their neighborhoods because of the rising crime rate, and that the fear of crime was beginning to erode the quality of our life as a nation.

I am, and always have been, an uncompromising advocate of a crackdown on crime and the causes of crime. I have directed my state administration so strongly and sharply against crime that I have been accused, at least in the most recent gubernatorial election campaign, of attempting to exploit the issue. I will rest on a newspaper description of the impact of crime in one neighborhood:

> The dread of crime has lately fallen like a blight over the Bronx neighborhood in which a 69-year-old retired bail bondsman was stabbed to death by a mugger on Monday afternoon.
>
> It has altered commerce and residential life in the Morrisania section, turning what had long been a quiet, friendly, safe area into one where people are acting and living more and more by their fears.
>
> Nearly every one in the section seemed able to tell a story yesterday of frightening and direct experience with crime.
>
> For some, the measures of defense are those of timidity —a cautious shrinking from dangers, real and imagined, behind their doors. They bar their windows, double- or triple-lock their doors, close their stores early, and walk the streets at night only with deliberation, if at all.
>
> Others are bold and angry. A few keep rifles and shotguns handy. There is talk of vigilante methods in the neighborhood.
>
> There are four drugstores within two blocks of the building in which the latest stabbing occurred. All four had long histories of crimeless years, lately broken by repeated robberies and break-ins. Proprietors believe narcotics addicts have marked the section for their crimes.

Crime drains the national economy by $27 billion of nonproductive expenditure every year. This comprises $22 billion or so in property losses, higher insurance rates, increased welfare and other budgets, and other indirect costs of crime, plus the $5 billion annual bill for our crime control partners, the police, the courts, the prisons and the parole authorities.

More than 30 percent of business failures in the nation are brought about by employee dishonesty—"white collar crime." Crime syndicates are increasingly invading legitimate real estate, banking, hotel and motel, garment manufacturing and other business and industrial interests. Only rarely does this invasion surface: A national magazine recently reported how racketeers attempted to pressure a supermarket chain into selling a certain type of detergent by bombing five supermarkets and murdering two store managers.

Our people are also clearly redefining what is a crime, and what is not, in their own personal lives. One luxury hotel in New York City reported recently that, after ten months in business, it had lost

- 38,000 demitasse spoons,
- 18,000 towels,
- 355 coffee pots and 500 bowls,
  Plus more than 100 Bibles.

The murderous edge of the crime crisis is, of course, narcotics addiction. Nationwide, drug law violations have increased by 82 percent over the past six years. In New York City, half the major crimes against property are committed by addicts who need to steal or attack to get the money for drugs.

The facts of the crime situation are so clear—and my

position is so clear—that I will limit my thoughts on the problem to detailing some of the steps I have taken as Governor of New York, and some others that I have recommended in the state and the nation.

We must, of course, root out the social conditions that breed and favor crime. But efforts at prevention are not enough—not when we have a chronic national infection of increasing criminality. In this context, we have got to improve the quality of our law enforcement agencies and the administration of justice. And we have got to enroll, train and pay enough men to do the crime-fighting job. The nation needs more than 50,000 new police officers, right now, to keep the situation under control. I have urged the national Administration to help close the gap by granting draft deferments to young men who wanted to begin an uninterrupted life's career in police work—a suggestion that was referred for study to the Advisory Committee on Selective Service, and is still being studied.

In New York State, we can take some pride in the fact that we have initiated and tested many of the recommendations of the President's Commission on Law Enforcement and the Administration of Justice by anticipating the problems in advance, in addition to adopting many new ideas of our own. With the close cooperation and assistance of the State Legislature, whether controlled by Democrats or Republicans, or divided, I have attempted to strengthen state and local law enforcement by reorganizing and greatly strengthening the state police, establishing a computer network for criminal identification, enacting "stop and frisk" and "no knock" legislation to help the police, and by launching the most comprehensive program in the nation to fight narcotics addiction and rehabilitate addicts.

We convened the state's first conference on crime in thirty years, bringing the best minds in government and private agencies to bear on the problems. We also continued to support a bipartisan state commission of investigation, and established a school of criminal justice in the State University.

I have acted to encourage the 600 or so separate police departments in New York State to consolidate where feasible, and to share such services as detective bureaus which cannot be manned satisfactorily by small forces. I am seeking to increase the state police force by several hundred additional men, and to require that district attorneys be full-time employees in larger counties. We plan a state study to determine the practicality, and the humaneness, of using new nonlethal weapons, under appropriate safeguards, in civil disorders.

I am also in favor of the use of wiretaps and electronic surveillance—among our most effective methods of combatting organized crime—under the civil-liberties safeguards laid down by the U.S. Supreme Court in the precedent-setting test case.

Again with the cooperation and assistance of the State Legislature, I have attempted to deal more effectively with criminal offenders—and to cut down the repeat offender rate—by broadening state aid to local probation services, improving parole supervision, and by authorizing a residential treatment facility, or "halfway house," to provide a bridge between the offender's total supervision in prison or reformatory and his return to the community under parole.

We have enacted legislation to provide "certificates of relief from disability" for certain first offenders, and we created the nation's most comprehensive program for the legal defense of indigent persons charged with crime.

Our new State Division for Youth has established a wide range of facilities and services for the rehabilitation of youngsters who are *on the brink of* delinquency, *in advance of* any formal trouble with the law. These include: Youth Division Homes, designed to provide a wholesome, home environment for troubled youngsters; Forestry Camps, where offenders live and work in state parks and conservation areas; and Short-Term Adolescent Training Centers, specializing in group discussions of problems. Our Short-Term Aid to Youth program allows young people, although failing to meet the requirements of behavior on probation, to remain at home under closer supervision. Our Hometown Beautification program enabled 3,000 young people to help us restore the scenic beauty around their communities last summer under state and local administration. Our record in rehabilitation of offenders of all ages is one in which we take pride.

In our continuing effort to head off youth crime before it starts, we have created a special, school-to-employment program to provide part-time jobs for fifteen-year-old boys in danger of dropping out of school. We set up a youth employment service as a special branch of the State Labor Department to help find jobs for sixteen-, seventeen- and eighteen-year-olds, established nine youth centers statewide. Into this partnership, we have also brought 3,000 4-H Clubs, among others, in a major move to help school dropouts with counseling and guidance. We have also started a variety of programs to give specialized training and cultural aid for gifted but underprivileged boys and girls.

There is no greater or more crucial task for a free nation than to prepare its youth—especially its troubled and disadvantaged youth—for citizenship in a democracy. A generation of free citizens that fails to look beyond itself is only preparing the death of its society. These young citizens are our hope for the future, our greatest living resource. Our basic goal in this field must be to see to it that all of our young people have the opportunity to fulfill their potential. These are undertakings of a high order in terms of human values.

New York State has been beset for many years with the grave problem of narcotics addiction and resultant crime. It is the principal point of entry for drugs of all descriptions. It is the state of domicile of 47 percent of our country's recorded, active addicts. It is an appalling situation—nothing to laugh at or argue away as a passing phase of our social and moral development. For this is a direct threat to the physical and mental health of hundreds of thousands of people.

Narcotics addiction eats up self-respect, destroys self-reliance, ravages the human body and undermines the value of life. Unlike other major diseases, drug addiction is primarily an illness of the young. Some 85 percent of addicts are under forty years of age, and 49 percent are under thirty. Adolescents and young adults are victimized before they are old enough and aware enough to appreciate the tragic consequences. Once "hooked," if they have nowhere to turn, they usually take to crime for money to buy drugs.

New York State has launched an all-out attack on narcotics addiction, removing narcotics addicts from the streets, placing them in mandatory confinement, rendering narcotics peddlers liable to harsh prison sentences, and expanding treatment and rehabilitation facilities in clinics and aftercare units within the community. We are treating more than 6,000 addicts this year and we expect to provide facilities for 15,000 addicts through new construction and joint use of clinical facilities with New York City and various private agencies. As I said in a message to the State Legislature, "You and I have a commitment to get these addicts off our streets. . . . We must not, we shall not, permit any obstacle to prevent our fulfilling this commitment."

I should also like to develop a clinical approach toward alcoholism. A study of one county penitentiary showed that 63 percent of the men there were imprisoned for offenses linked in one way or another to alcohol. Every casual visitor to almost any crowded courtroom is familiar with the pathetic lines of drunks. Why should these men be sent to prison if they have committed no serious offenses? They are sick and should be in clinics—where the resources of the community may be brought to bear to help them solve their own problems if that is possible.

Finally, I would like to make far greater inroads into

the problem of violence as such, specifically meaning firearms control. I have a rifle—and I have no objection to getting a license to possess it. I also have a pistol—and I had no objection to getting a license for that. I see no legitimate reason why any responsible, law-abiding hunter, antique firearms collector, or gun-owner of any persuasion and hobby should object to firearms controls designed to keep guns away from demented, irresponsible or lawless people.

Early one December evening not long ago, in Bryant Park, behind the New York City Public Library, a former mental patient got up from a bench and calmly started firing away with a rifle. Two people fell dead and it was a miracle that the loss of life was not higher. The man had bought the rifle and the ammunition just one hour before from a gun shop four blocks away.

The reason such senseless tragedies occur is that our gun control laws, though more stringent than most other states' laws, are frankly inadequate. I presented a Safe Gun program to the State Legislature this year. Unfortunately, it met the usual fate of such measures. Most safe-gun legislation rarely gets anywhere because the lobbying efforts of some sporting organizations and other groups opposed to firearms controls are highly effective. An implied argument of the gun lobby is that safe-gun legislation is somehow intended to disarm the people—that guns are going to be confiscated or outlawed. This is not true. A professional survey of New York citizens has revealed that 82 percent favor registration of firearms—a finding confirmed by similar Gallup Poll results on the national level. President Johnson has rightly condemned "mail order murder" in his attempts to impose more effective federal controls over guns sold and shipped through the mail—guns like the Mannlicher-Carcano used by Lee Harvey Oswald to assassinate President Kennedy. As a single state, there is not much that we can do about interstate mailing of firearms. But I believe that my safe-gun program would go far to curb and control the over-the-counter traffic in murder in New York State. Sooner or later, it will be law.

I am in total accord with those who insist that the way to fight crime is to cure the social ills in which desperation breeds. But I also want to put criminals under control, under care, on the road to rehabilitation, rather than let them continue to roam the streets and parks, to rob, to assault, and sometimes to kill. I want to make our streets safe again. I want to check the rising tide of crime. I want to restore thousands of our young men to happy and useful lives. I yield to no man in my determination to eradicate the slums. But crime is something else.

V

HEALTH &

EDUCATION

A human being has the right to security in cases of sickness, inability to work, widowhood, old age, unemployment, or in any other case in which he is deprived of the means of subsistence through no fault of his own.

Once this is admitted, it is also clear that, in human society, to one man's right, there corresponds a duty in all other persons; the duty, namely, of acknowledging and respecting the right in question, and that each contribute generously to the establishment of a civic order in which rights and duties are progressively, more sincerely and effectively acknowledged and fulfilled.

—Pope John XXIII

Man is still the greatest miracle and the greatest problem on this earth.

—David Sarnoff

Sixteen years ago, when General Eisenhower received the Republican nomination for the Presidency, he asked me to head a committee to study and recommend changes in the organization of the federal government. This experience led me to the deep, personal conviction, shared by the other members of the committee, that the elements of human concern facing the nation should be elevated to the highest levels of government and given Cabinet status. At this time, one of the most helpful persons to me and to the committee was the late Senator Robert A. Taft, an authority and humanitarian in the fields of health, education, transportation and public housing.

Shortly after his election, President Eisenhower formalized our committee and endorsed our recommendation by setting up the Department of Health, Education, and Welfare. President Eisenhower and the first Secretary of the new department, Mrs. Oveta Culp Hobby of Houston, the wartime director of the Women's Army Corps, asked me to serve as Under Secretary. My first order of business was to commence an overall review of the Social Security program that had been founded during the New Deal. As a result, I participated in the development of a series of amendments to the Social Security Law—the most extensive ever enacted—and their presentation to the Congress. These amendments, enacted in 1954, extended Social Security coverage to ten million more of our people and increased benefits 20 to 30 percent, which was the largest increase ever enacted.

Social Security, with its many facets, has proven to be a most significant bulwark of individual dignity and family pride. Anybody who contends otherwise simply does not understand human beings—and does not realize what Social Security benefits mean every month to widows, to the dependents of deceased and disabled workers, to young men and women who would otherwise have to support as well as honor their fathers and mothers unto death. The compulsory nature of Social Security in effect guarantees the 20 million recipients—and the 63 million who anticipate benefits on retirement—that their pay checks will not be stopped. Were the system to be made voluntary, the danger is that enough young people who felt they did not need protection would foolishly opt out of Social Security and so the system would collapse. Social Security provides a "floor of protection" on which individual thrift and initiative can build. Experience has shown that Social Security has given impetus to individual life insurance and retirement plans, and to group pension plans, providing millions of workers with additional protection for the retirement years.

While a consensus has long supported Social Security, a titanic struggle has been waged across our country for and against Medicare. This is essentially a mandatory, contributory hospital insurance plan for people over sixty-five under Social Security. At the time I served in HEW, I tried to convince private insurance companies to agree to a federal reinsurance pool so that they would be in a better position to write catastrophic health insurance. I was deeply troubled that the vast majority of our people lacked this protection against catastrophic illness. Every year, about 3 percent of all Americans were being forced into actual bankruptcy because medical expenses for illnesses late in life were consuming their savings.

The Census Bureau estimated that 52 percent of Americans over sixty-five had incomes of less than $1,000 per year, and only 6.3 percent had incomes of more than $5,000 a year. A survey taken as late as 1960 showed that 30 percent of those over sixty-five had no liquid assets, that only 40 percent had more than $2,000, and inflation, the deadly enemy, was sapping even those slender defenses. As a Miami doctor put it:

"An aged person can usually pay for his first illness out of his savings. On his second illness, he mortgages his home. After the third, he goes on the county."

A spokesman for the Golden Rule, a club for older people, said, "Our people have two alternatives—one is, get rich, but it is too late in the game, and the other is, get poor, and the welfare will take care of you."

I was moved by the story of the oldest living man in the United States, a proud former slave named Charlie Smith, who ran a refreshment stand at his two-room home outside Polk City, Fla. For 119 of his 120 years, Smith's boast was, "I ain't never been sick, I never took a dose of medicine, and I ain't never been in a hospital." But one morning Smith woke up feeling poorly, and he walked into town to see the doctor, who diagnosed prostate trouble and prescribed hospital treatment at an estimated cost of $500. "I don't have five hundred dollars," the old man said, simply. Hours later, he was admitted to the Polk County Hospital for indigents at the county seat of Bartow. He had come face to face with the problem haunting the lives of our 18.5 million citizens of sixty-five and over—how to pay medical bills without liquidation of their self-respect.

My own considerable interest in the situation—and my passionate support of Medicare—derived logically enough from my upbringing in the shadow of the Rockefeller Foundation. This philanthropic organization deployed the best medical talent it could find against hookworm in the South, yellow fever in Ecuador, scarlet fever in Romania, dengue fever in Guam, malaria in Nicaragua. My own first entry into public life was as a member of the Westchester County Board of Health, an active membership that continued for twenty years.

Increasingly, I found myself preoccupied with the historic question, posed subsequently to the whole world by Pope John XXIII, whether mankind in fact possessed "a right to security." I learned that the problem of providing medical care for those who are neither rich enough to pay for what they need, nor poor enough to claim charity, was a classical one; and out of historical understanding, I strengthened my point of view.

In Britain in the eighteenth century, for example, Huguenot workers banded together in voluntary insurance societies—aptly named "friendly societies"—and semireligious organizations such as the Ancient Order of Foresters took on a similar role. These voluntary programs were a natural complement to the philanthropic hospitals, often operated by churches, which were supported openhandedly by conscientious merchants who followed Wesley's dictum: "Gain all you can. Save all you can. Give all you can." But as the Industrial Revolution swept the Western world, the dislocations among the working classes were severe. The poor farm or the debtor's prison were often the best that the homeless, jobless, and aged of the day could hope for. It was an era that fed the fiction of Dickens

—and Marx. And it was an age that saw the gradual development of institutions, such as labor unions, that perceived medical care to be a legitimate objective of social action.

The role of government in medicine was largely confined to preventive measures until the middle of the nineteenth century when Germany, under the Iron Chancellor, Prince Otto von Bismarck, became the first modern nation to pass comprehensive legislation providing its citizens with medical care. Between 1882 and 1889, the Reichstag passed three major laws to provide compulsory health insurance and other benefits for workmen, setting a fabulous array of precedents that ranged from half-and-half sharing of premium payments between employers and employees to the formal definition of age sixty-five as that appropriate for retirement. Bismarck abhorred socialism—in 1878 he outlawed the "Social Democratic Party"—but he wanted to improve the lot of the poor. Majestically he declared, "No doubt, the individual can do much good, but the social problem can only be solved by the state. The state is not merely a necessary but a beneficent institution."

Bismarck's enlightenment left its mark not only on Germany—the present West German social insurance program is a direct descendant—but on all the industrial nations of the West. Britain set up a medical care program in 1911 to provide limited insurance for low-income workers. In the United States, Theodore Roosevelt's Bull Moose party called for "the protection of home life against the hazards of sickness, irregular employment and old age through the adoption of a system of social insurance adapted to American use." It was the first time a U.S. political party had gone so far in proposing social legislation.

But fiery old Samuel Gompers, the great labor leader, was adamantly opposed to the idea of compulsory medical insurance—"undemocratic—and it cannot remove or prevent poverty," he said. At the same time, the American Medical Association actually favored the idea. In 1917, the AMA House of Delegates said that doctors would be left "in a position of helplessness if the rising tide of social development sweeps over them. In the end, the social forces that demand these laws will indignantly force a recalcitrant profession to accept that which is unjust to it, and that which is to its detriment."

But the AMA reversed itself (as did Gompers' American Federation of Labor) and briefly opposed not only medicare but private insurance plans such as Blue Cross and, as the AMA then said, "a considerable number of businessmen who see in various insurance and other commercial medical schemes an opportunity for recouping fortunes lost through other business ventures."

On the other hand, the AMA did not oppose the Social Security Act in the midst of the unbelievable pressures and hardships of the New Deal.

After World War II, Great Britain took its drastic and only partly successful steps toward socialized medicine which, despite administrative chaos and a probable decline in medical standards, is still popular among the people.

Speaker of the House of Representatives Sam Rayburn, no enthusiast for Medicare, changed his mind on the sub-

ject when his brother Tom died of cancer after a long illness. Mr. Sam paid the bills. "I had the money and was
glad to do it," he said. "But a lot of folks don't have the
money, and can't do it."

The struggle over Medicare was still raging at the federal level when I was elected Governor of New York in
1958. Medicare was not, in fact, to be enacted until 1965.
One of my first moves as Governor was to study the feasi-
bility of a state-run prepaid health system to protect all
New Yorkers against catastrophic medical bills. This
proved to be an idea whose time had not come, and we
were unable to obtain action on the plan, especially because it would have placed New York industry at a com-
petitive disadvantage in the absence of similar actions by
other states.

But we did establish the nation's most comprehensive
medical assistance plan for the aged, and we authorized
localities to give 50 percent property tax relief on homes
owned by persons aged sixty-five with incomes of $3,000
or less. We tripled the number of state-aided housing
units, completed and started, for the aged, and we provided
100 percent development loans to nonprofit groups for
housekeeping units for the aged under our middle-income
private housing plan. We increased—sevenfold—state aid
to localities that agreed to operate recreational programs
for the elderly, and we granted 100 percent real estate tax
exemption to nonprofit groups sponsoring special housing
for old people. We also created a new State Office for the
Aging. And when the federal government began its medical assistance to the aged under the Kerr-Mills plan, our
state came up with the largest, most liberal program in the

nation. Under that program, our sick and needy senior citizens received more than 25 percent of the money spent through Kerr-Mills in the United States.

As Governor, I made the people's health a first order of business, and my associates and I achieved results that strengthened my personal philosophy. Where we found state rehabilitation aid confined to needy children with orthopedic defects, we included those suffering from such chronic ills as diabetes, leukemia, cystic fibrosis, asthma, cancer and epilepsy. Today, more than 18,000 children receive benefits from this program—a 150 percent increase. We also authorized a Birth Defects Institute to conduct research into causes and possible treatment of birth defects. Where we found that the disabled often lacked rehabilitation facilities, we began a statewide network of rehabilitation centers, twenty-three of which are now in operation, with eleven more planned. We set up a new Heart Disease Bureau, supported heart research in Albany, Buffalo and New York City, and trained more than 6,000 medical personnel in new resuscitation techniques. Where we found no controls over unqualified clinical laboratories, and over potentially lethal X-ray equipment, we insisted that laboratories be licensed, X-ray equipment inspected, and X-ray technicians licensed. Where we found an alarming decline in the ratio of doctors to patients, we decided to expand a third state medical school at Buffalo and created a fourth at Stony Brook.

Upon my recommendation, the Legislature provided ample funds to train 130 doctors a year, under contracts with private medical schools—the equivalent to setting up a new medical school. We also established a $700 million program of low-interest loans for the construction of new public hospitals and modernization of existing municipal facilities.

Our greatest progress was made in the area of mental health. Out of our Master Plan for meeting the challenge of mental disability—the first in the nation—we created a Mental Hygiene Facilities Improvement Fund to construct a massive $600 million of new mental health facilities. These included five new hospitals with a total of 2,400 beds for the mentally ill, ten new schools with a capacity of 7,000 for the mentally retarded, nine new facilities with a capacity of 1,200 for emotionally disturbed children and fifteen new rehabilitation centers for the mentally ill.

If my life in the public service were to end tomorrow, I would find comfort—I would believe this made it all worthwhile—in our great gains in mental health. We provided new facilities for 11,000 mentally disabled patients, opening the first new State Mental Hospital and State School for the Retarded since the 1930's, and we increased state funds for mental health by more than 70 percent. We more than doubled the staffs in the state schools, augmented the staff-to-patient ratio from one staff member to 3.4 patients in 1959 to one to 1.7, and we increased staff salaries by 55 percent. At the same time, we more than tripled state aid for the operation of community mental health services in our belief that mentally ill people can often be treated more effectively close to home. And by improving our methods for the treatment of the mentally ill, and humanizing admission laws, we succeeded in reducing the average stay of persons in mental hospitals from eight months in 1958 to approximately sixty-seven days now.

Essentially, I accepted the experience that medical care was a demonstrable, individual good. I absorbed the lessons of history that it was also a social need. I therefore turned increasingly to the pragmatic question of how best to deliver it for the most people.

As I have said, President Johnson obtained the passage of Medicare in 1965—history may rate this his greatest accomplishment. To this bill, Congress tacked on an additional section, Title XIX, offering Medicaid support out of public funds for citizens defined as medically indigent. New York State moved at once to obtain maximum benefits under these plans. And I grew increasingly convinced that we ought next to move, at the federal level if possible, and at the state level if not, toward a Universal Health Insurance system. This ought to be the first line of defense of health protection for everybody. No enlightened society will now, in the light of history, set ability to pay as a prerequisite of medical care. Therefore, publicly financed medicine does have a justified place by providing care for those who are indisputably poor or who cannot meet the costs of catastrophic illness.

However, the great failing of publicly paid medicine is that it contains no self-restraining force to curb excessive expansion and abuses—which we have seen in the administration of Medicaid. The beneficiaries do not contribute, financially, and thus have no personal stake in the fiscal solidity of the system. In addition, excessive expansion, powered by demagogues, could lead to socialized medicine. Contributory health insurance is, by contrast, most in keeping with the needs, wishes and traditions of the great majority of our people. Specifically, a Universal Health Insurance system will:

· Maintain the doctor-patient relationship without government intruding into a traditionally confidential area;

· Enable us to build on the existing and well-developed base of our present private and nonprofit health insurance companies, as well as our governmental operations;

· Avoid the reluctance some may feel about using medical programs even though they may be eligible and may need the care;

· Underscore an individual's self-reliance and enhance his personal dignity in time of trouble;

· Give beneficiaries a stake in the prudent management of the enterprise, if only because their premium rates will reflect the efficiency of management.

My sureness that Universal Health Insurance is the correct approach was fortified, recently, when the Congress cut back on federal aid to the states for Medicaid, incidentally breaking the federal government's original promise of support for the states. Congress' move is costing New York State $43 million in federal aid in the first year and $61 million in the second. The federal cutback in

Medicaid left us with the alternatives of rolling back Medicaid or putting up more state and local money at higher tax cost to our citizens. I made repeated recommendations to the federal government not to break faith with the states on Medicaid. But these pending federal actions sharply reinforced my desire for Universal Health Insurance—not to "bail out" Medicaid but because, in the long run, health insurance is a far sounder way to finance health care.

My belief in Universal Health Insurance in America also reflects the simple reality that we must have better management of the hospitals, in particular, if we are not to be swamped with problems, especially problems of soaring costs. Nowhere is the rising cost of living more apparent than in the hospitals of our state: in 1950, the average cost of a room was $10.72 per day; in 1960, it was $21.33; today, it is $43.38. The improvement of the care brings escalating costs. An intensive coronary care unit today costs about $450,000 to install and equip, and about $150 per day to maintain a single patient there. Recently, I read how a hyperbaric chamber saved a young man with gas gangrene from near-certain death. In its daylong, nightlong struggles to save many lives, the hospital must pay an installation cost of a hyperbaric chamber of approximately $750,000 plus an additional $207,000 per year to maintain it.

I was impressed, like everybody else, by the photograph of Philip Blaiberg walking out of a hospital in South Africa with someone else's heart beating in his breast—but it costs our hospitals about $250,000 just to go into open heart surgery and another $200,000 per year to maintain it. These sophisticated and expensive advances, along with rising hospital payrolls and maintenance costs, help to explain the relentless economic pressures today.

Therefore, as Governor of New York, I have proposed a Health Security Act to our State Legislature. This is designed to meet two critical objectives:

1. To make mandatory, contributory health insurance, financed through employer and employee contributions, that will insure protection to virtually all of the state's population under sixty-five years of age (Medicare already is in force to cover those over sixty-five);

2. To make the hospital's rate of reimbursement from the state dependent and conditional upon its management efficiency so that good management practices can be rewarded and poor management penalized.

The basic service benefits mandated by this bill—this Universal Health Insurance—would provide for 120 days of semiprivate, in-hospital care, including maternity, psychiatric and ancillary services, plus 100 days of home care, plus hospital out-patient diagnostic services and out-patient care for accidental injury or emergency illness.

The bill would require the state to contribute to the cost of health benefits when the combined contribution of employer and employee exceeds four percent of the employer's annual payroll. Employee contributions in no case would exceed 2 percent of wages or one-half the cost of providing coverage, whichever was less. Persons who are unemployed, on public assistance, or eligible for medical assistance would have their health insurance purchased for them by the state, with federal and local participation.

Under the proposed program, state agencies and health insurers would pay for hospital services only at rates certified by the state.

The proposed Health Security Act also contains built-in management incentives by offering, for example, better reimbursement rates to hospitals that agree to pool central services in their areas. Hospitals that do not wish to merge these services would have to maintain them at their own expense.

The Health Security Act would exclude from reimbursement any professional service not fully required by the demand, such as salary and equipment costs that appear to be lavish, or duplicated. It would also tie the reimbursement rates to the trend of the state and national economy and cost of living and to costs in comparable hospitals. Because adequate and uniform financial information regarding hospital costs is essential in dealing with the problem, the Health Security Act would require the state to set up uniform and statewide cost-accounting and cost-analysis systems for all hospitals. We must put an end to the present situation in which hospitals are operating more or less on a cost-plus economy. One survey in New York State reported that twenty-two voluntary hospitals were charging from $50 to $87 per day for similar services, and we have all heard about, and read about, similar discrepancies.

This is a most serious business. Health care, along with adequate education, is one of the indispensables for our people if they are to know the opportunities of our way of life. Good hospital care is not an individual privilege, dependent upon financial means. It is a basic human right in today's society. This condition confronts responsible public officials with inescapable alternatives: we may ignore the hardship created by rising medical costs; we may expand the expensive and inefficient Medicaid-type systems of public medicine; or else, we may make the decision to guarantee *all* of our people a first line of health defense under Universal Health Insurance, strengthened by hospital cost controls.

I have seen contributory health insurance succeed in the case of Medicare. I have seen the serious shortcomings of Medicaid, of medical care financed out of tax revenues. Therefore, I have now urged the federal government to enact a program of national, universal, health insurance—coupled with hospital cost controls—as a first order of public affairs. This could be one of the decisive steps forward of the final third of the century and I intend to press for it with all my energy and will.

As to education, I vowed when I became Governor that every one of our 6,000,000 young people would have an equal opportunity for an education to the limit of his or her desires and ability. A sound education is the key that unlocks the door to advancement in every field of human effort. As Governor, I found that almost all of our citizens were in accord on the objectives and differed only on detail. So I found that my best service was to be what our Polish citizens call a *"dobry gospodarz,"* a good manager. Studies showed that the private institutions of higher education in New York could not meet in time, or in degree, the critical need for college facilities arising from the rapid postwar increase in the birthrate and in the demand for educated manpower. It was equally clear that a large-scale expansion of the State University and the City University of New York was imperative as a matter of public policy. It was likewise inevitable that the historic pattern of our private colleges and universities would be deeply affected. A similar trend was inevitable in primary and secondary education. The statistics best tell the story.

In Primary and Secondary Education, we:

· Raised state aid to public schools to $1.8 billion, an increase of 227 percent, to handle an increased enrollment of 26 percent;

· Initiated a reform of the state school-aid formula to give special financial aid to hard-pressed city school districts and sparsely settled rural districts, and established for the first time state financial aid to city school districts for transportation;

· Raised teachers' salaries by 30 percent, increased pensions and expanded in-service training and refresher courses for teachers, offered quadrupled state aid for libraries and developed a statewide educational television network;

· Established a new program of state aid designed to make modern vocational training available to young people in all parts of the state.

In Higher Education, we:

· Transformed the State University into the fastest-growing in the world, increasing enrollment from 38,000 students when I took office to 140,000 in 1968, on a projection that will bring it 185,000 students or more by 1970;

· Increased the State University faculty by 3,000 teachers, at higher salary levels, and launched a $1.5 billion construction program to handle the expansion;

· Increased state aid to the City University of New York by more than 600 percent;

· Created the Scholar Incentive Program to give financial awards for more than 206,000 students in public and private universities at a cost of $34 million, while quadrupling the number of Regents scholarships, and guaranteeing student loans to more than 100,000 students (the figure was 5,266 when I took office) at no interest during college and 3 percent after graduation;

· Nearly tripled state aid to community colleges and maintained support for private colleges in our continuing quest for diversity and excellence in education.

VI

THE ROLES
OF WOMEN

Although Susan B. Anthony was born in Massachusetts, the Governor of New York traditionally sets
aside February 15th of every year to commemo-
rate her effective work in the nineteenth century for freedom, justice and equality for women. She was an agent of
the American Anti-Slavery Society in New York before she
began to agitate for women's rights. Her motto was: "The
true republic—men, their rights and nothing more; women,
their rights and nothing less." Her work led directly to the
adoption of the Nineteenth Amendment to the Constitution, providing votes for women. Courage of a rare sort
indeed was needed to bring her and her associates through

the hostility—and the ridicule—they encountered as they set forth to change our history and succeeded.

I often wondered, as I signed the Susan B. Anthony Day proclamation, whether women yet contribute adequately to the solution of our national and community problems, and whether our several governments were doing all they could to help them make this contribution. Presidents, governors and mayors are asked this question until sometimes it seems tiresome—and yet it is true. The plain fact is—and one of the little-measured opportunities of the next decade—that we can do very much more to tap the skills, the knowledge, and the human values of women for the national purpose. Only 7 percent of our doctors are women, only 3 percent of our lawyers are women, only 2 percent of our dentists are women. Until recently out of all 1,495 presidents of our universities and four-year colleges, only 117 were women—and all but eight of these 117 were presidents of all-women's educational institutions of religious orientation and endowment.

Measuring women's contribution to the decision-making processes of our private enterprise system—especially, management and labor leadership—is even more revealing. Outside New York City, Chicago, Los Angeles and Washington, D.C., hardly any working women earn more than $12,000 a year from their jobs. I have personally signed, sealed and delivered laws providing for equal rights and equal pay for equal jobs, but have been able to do little about the invisible pay line, drawn by men, beyond which women do not rise. Women tend to do better in government, incidentally, and about one in ten of our state executives is a woman making more than $12,000 a year.

According to one successful New York woman, "a good part of women's problems in their professional lives have been caused by women themselves. They have let it be known that they have trouble working with and for other women. They have spread the word that women who work lose their femininity. What we therefore need is to demonstrate that motherhood and brainpower can go, and in fact do go, together very well."

I would add, first, that our national problems are looming so large that the United States can no longer afford not to ask women to help—and make it possible for them to help—and provide incentives for them to help.

I would add, secondly, that there are many areas that are wholly suited for women to move into and, perhaps, take over. I am thinking, for example, of the great good they could accomplish in meeting the environmental crisis —the problems of air and water pollution, depletion of natural resources, adulteration of food and drugs. Women, too, could take the lead in assuring real protection for consumers, in supporting and stimulating the arts at the community level—and in many other fields.

One of the difficulties of this issue of a new role for women is, of course, that too few take it seriously. One journalist of my acquaintance once quipped, "We'll take care of the women after we get the Negroes' problems squared away." Another difficulty is that the significance of the situation has been obscured—I might add, clogged up—by the sludge of second-rate sociology to which we have all been subjected. Women have been depicted as enduring the horrors of "quiet desperation" and "extreme frustration" when most are coping intelligently with the complex pressures of busy lives, managing to be companionable wives and understanding mothers, responsible members of the community and usually well-informed spectators and occasional participants in public life.

I know from the evidence of my own voting analysis records that women overwhelmingly supported our $1.7 billion Pure Waters Program designed to eliminate water pollution in the state in six years. I know they provided more than the measure of victory for our $2.5 billion Transportation Bond Issue when we needed it.

When I established our first, permanent Bureau of Consumer Frauds and Protection, under the direction of our State Attorney General, Louis Lefkowitz, I needed the help of women to make it work. In one year alone, in New York City alone, we were able to start ten thousand investigations and lawsuits, and we were able to return $1.2 million to dissatisfied customers, because women believed that the new Bureau meant what it said, and took the time and trouble to bring abuses to our attention. Lefkowitz reports we now have "five or six housewives in every county of the state, acting as the eyes and ears of our office."

The prime fact of the matter, however, is this: The biggest single change in American employment in the past ten years has been the increase in the numbers of married women at work. As recently as 1950, only one in five of the married women living with their husbands was working for a living. Today, it is one in three—a statistic of staggering significance. This is in fact a social change almost as profound as the migration of hundreds of thousands of Negroes from the South to the Northern industrial cities, and it is, as yet, scarcely noted or understood. I therefore convened a Special Committee on the Education and Employment of Women, under the chairmanship of Mrs. Oswald B. Lord, formerly one of the U.S. delegates to the United Nations, and, subsequently, a Governor's Conference on Women, under the chairmanship of Mrs. Kitty Carlisle Hart, designed to develop the facts upon which we can begin to plan to enlist more women in the national interest. I am deeply indebted to these groups for their vital groundwork; they have established the basis of an opportunity for our country which I intend to develop to the utmost.

These facts about women in New York State are applicable, in general, to women nationwide:

Of all women, 58 percent are married, 22 percent are single, and 20 percent are widowed, divorced or separated. One in three of all employed persons is a woman. As women reach different age levels, the proportion of women workers, of course, changes, and during the child-bearing years only one woman in three is still working. But, and this is the great change, between ages thirty-five to forty-four, the percentage of women working increases to 43 percent and, between forty-five to fifty-four, to one in two, an employment of women almost as great as that to be found in the traditional career-girl years of eighteen to twenty-four.

None of this downgrades the essential role of women in the family and in the home and, as Mrs. Romine Foster, president, New York State Congress of Parents and Teachers, put it, "I have a great deal of concern for the lack of prestige these days for being a mother. I think we must teach young girls in our schools to use their education in being very good mothers, in offering themselves to the community, in being knowledgeable in the fields of legislation and social welfare. Things need to be done right at the grass roots. Mothers can do them and be back home when the children come home from school." And, as Dr. Genevieve Loughran, Associate Professor of the Graduate Program in Guidance and School Counseling at Hunter College, added:

"Today's young girl expects to work until Prince Charming comes along and then to retire forever from the labor market. Nothing could be more unrealistic in view of the changing role of women."

Women, then, have several roles in life, and they are balancing them with increasing intelligence. They are devoting priority to their role in the family and in the home. And they are increasingly viewing their "work-life" as part of the mainstream of existence—to be entered into, suspended and then, perhaps, resumed, if they choose to, if they need the money, if they perceive an opportunity to make an individual contribution. In this multifaceted situation, the old concept of women *tied* to the home (*Kinder, Kirche, Küche*), represents a hopeless misunderstanding of the American way of life.

This is no longer a social question, to be admired or deplored, but a matter of fact, to be recognized and responded to. The role of government, I scarcely need to add, is to channel this hopeful new trend toward the national interest.

I want to turn women loose on the environmental crisis —and I think they can solve it better than men can—because they care more, because they are closer to it. Nobody knows more about pollution when detergents back up the kitchen sink—and when it is impossible to go out of doors in the city without getting your clothes filthy—and when you cannot take the children swimming in the rivers or the lakes because the waters are foul with pollution.

Women care deeply about these things—and women can do much to set them right if given the chance.

Dr. Esther M. Westervelt, Professor of Education at Teachers College, Columbia University, has these interesting thoughts on the role of women in public life:

"A very central theme is the problem of achieving womanhood in our society . . . of moving from the private to the public sphere and managing to keep and develop one's womanhood while one is doing this," she says. "Most of us are agreed that we need women in the public sphere in a society where most of our important work is done in the public sphere—not in spite of the fact that we are women, or because we are able to acquire the same skills that men can acquire, but because we are women and we bring feminine values to the public sector of work and thinking.

"We also talk about the problem of achieving self-fulfillment. What we mean by this has something to do with our cultural or ethnic background, and something to do with our economic advantages or disadvantages. The privileged, middle-class woman seeks self-fulfillment by an expression of her individuality in a variety of ways. And there is a very large group of women who do not have to decide whether or not to work for pay in order to express their individuality. They *have to work* for pay. Their problem is basically one of finding work for pay which is also personally rewarding and which fits with their domestic responsibilities.

"All of these women—at least, many of them—are encountering extremely serious problems and *before* they can play their part in national life, they need help."

To this, I would add that equality and greater fulfillment for women can neither be achieved by legislation alone nor necessarily be advanced by proof that they can match the competence and performance of men in most forms of achievement—and that the needs of women and the needs of society are served together by the utilization rather than the waste of women's talents and energies.

So, how to solve the problems:

• There is increasing demand for trained and talented women to go back to school or back to work. Yet it is harder and harder for these women to find capable help at home.

• A bright, educated woman with time on her hands but no specialized training may feel that her talents are underused, but she has no notion where to go, or even where to look, for guidance and retraining.

• Many women have a very real need to add to the family income. The competition for jobs is high, and this cost is augmented by the daily carrying charges—from lunches to transportation to babysitters—of the return to full-time work.

• There are increasing numbers of women whose training is outmoded by the rapid changes in our technology, particularly in those fields affected by automation, and there is a great need for retraining.

• As the number of people over fifty increases, there are many more older women—in fact, women in their sixties and seventies as well—who are able to perform needed functions but are discriminated against because of their age.

• There is pressure on women to expand their capabilities by vocational training and retraining, but there is little factual information on vocational needs of the future, and it is not outlandish to suggest that women might need to retrain several times in the course of their work lives.

• Everything will continue to depend upon the economic growth rate of the community and the country, and women (again, like Negroes) might be the first to be laid off in times of economic downdraft.

There is already a greater variety of voluntary work available than ever before. This will be one of the ways in which women will be able to work against social ills most effectively. But volunteer work will increasingly need more than willing hearts, and good neighbors may find they will have to become skilled and trained demographers, designers, transportation planners, sanitation specialists, community historians, theatrical producers, schedulers, surveyors, population planners *if they are to be* effective and useful volunteers.

These problems, though sizable, are of relatively small stature compared to the virtually overwhelming historical trends. As my Special Committee on Women's Education and Employment reported, "With the number and variety of ways available for the continuation of education—with the numbers of women pouring into, and pouring back into, the labor market—with the new flexibility of school and work hours adjusted to women's double responsibilities of home and professional life—with changes gradually taking place in the discrimination against the employment and the promotion of women—it looks as if, in our generation, we may be nearing a milestone comparable to the admission of women to institutions of higher learning in the mid-nineteenth century, or even to the passage of the Women's Suffrage Amendment."

How can people in government, such as myself, help in the guidance, retraining and continuing education of women who may at some time return to the labor force?

What can we do to open up opportunities to women and make known to employers the availability of qualified women?

What long-range measures may we undertake, at all

levels of our society, to widen opportunities for women in all sectors of public life?

I am convinced that we need an action program on women's education to qualify millions of people to play a new and vital part in our national development and pursuit of happiness. We need an action program on women's employment to improve our country's utilization of women workers, women's skills and women's values. And we need an action program on opportunities for women, to eliminate discriminatory laws and practices and invisible barriers to the acceptance and employment and promotion of women—with enforcement procedures to ensure that women do in fact get an equal chance.

My first suggestion would be the convening of a national educational congress to explore the changing roles of women and to shape new educational patterns for the future. A woman's life goals are the product of her environment—the total result of her education from preschool and kindergarten onward. These should be revised and readjusted in the light of our new information about women's prospects. It is not too early to explain, even in grade school, that girls will grow up not only to be married and have children but that they will have activities and responsibilities outside the home. Grade school and high school are not too soon for very thorough and realistic vocational training. At the other end of the educational spectrum, it is important to establish that, in today's world, graduation is not terminal, and that women must maintain their job skills and refresh them periodically. The educational congress should point to the limitations affecting the acceptance of women in professional schools and industrial training courses—the number of women engineers in our country is currently heading downward, incidentally—and see that changes are made.

My second suggestion would be to expand, nationwide, a vital program of part-time study courses and home-study courses to enable married women to continue their education, if necessary, at home. These courses would be set up in cooperation with secondary schools, community colleges and state universities to qualify hundreds of thousands of women for high school diplomas, college proficiency examinations, degrees, and simply to enable them to maintain their own education for their own personal sense of fulfillment.

My third suggestion would be to organize the re-employment of married women around pilot community guidance centers. These would be set up within communities to help women evaluate their capabilities, at all ages, to suggest where and how they can obtain any training and retraining they may need, and to have available lists of suitable employment opportunities. The guidance centers would also serve as clearinghouses for information about volunteer work available, in addition to existing sources, and as a helpful channel through which local employers might be able to learn about qualified women needing useful work.

My fourth suggestion is the creation of professional reserves. By this I mean, for example, that a teacher who retires to have children is not to be lost to the teaching profession, but is to be placed on a Teachers' Reserve.

There, for ten, twenty, or more years, she is kept up to date on teaching developments and systems changes, informed on part-time teaching opportunities, addressed as an honored professional and not as a has-been, so that her professional skill is maintained as a community (and her own) resource. This professional reserve approach could be applicable to nurses, dieticians, home economists, specialized clerical personnel, specialized technical personnel, and could have a personal as well as professional usefulness. It is interesting to note, I believe, that several of our largest corporations are beginning to set up their own reserves of former employees—even conducting retraining classes and social gatherings for them—in the hope that the women will some day come back to perform useful work.

My fifth suggestion would be to attempt to define standards for professional certification and accreditation of homemakers' assistants. Once the stigma of the menial is lifted, household help will become more available, and as women advance to higher professional standards and salary levels, they will be able to afford household help more readily. Hopefully, it will be an ascending spiral. I realize that there will also have to be a much larger-gauge approach to the creation of community day-care centers—yet this too can be an ascending spiral as the status of nurses and certified assistants in these community day-care centers rises along with professional standards.

My sixth suggestion would be to develop a sustained system of fact-finding, such as that conducted by the women's committees in New York, to provide specific information on the performance of women in key positions, to show how industries and communities are using women employees effectively, to maintain records on the qualifications and talents of women who return to the labor market, to demonstrate the successes and lessons to be learned from community college and other training and retraining programs. I would attempt to dispel the mumbo-jumbo prejudices and suspicions of women workers that persist in our society to the national detriment. This new approach might even require major steps such as the formalization of permanent, regional and industrial commissions on womenpower. It might also require the establishment of a nationwide register of women qualified for high-level appointive posts, an extension of the present, helpful registers maintained by the National Council of Women and the American Association of University Women.

We should expand the volunteer work among American women that is an integral function of our national success, and that other nations seek, sometimes vainly, to emulate. There is absolutely no substitute for women, highly motivated, highly trained, almost literally policing their communities against abuse of any kind, almost literally writing the blueprints for progress and mustering up the voting power to see that they are enacted. By its very nature, this is a community priority. At one of the town meetings I held in New York State, a woman who had never been active in government raised a point that I was unable to answer: She said she lived in a community where we were building an express highway. A small swimming hole for the children had been an important community activity. But the state highway department put the highway through the area and, the woman told me, "You wouldn't believe it. At great expense, they trucked gravel for twelve miles to fill the swimming hole to grade the area. They could just as well have dug another swimming hole outside the area taken over by the state, taken the dirt from there, and put it in the first hole, and we would have a new swimming hole today." It was so offbeat, and yet so obvious, that I told the meeting: "Sure. That's a perfect example of why we need more women in government."

As Governor of New York, I have implemented several of my proposals on the enhanced role for women that I contemplate nationwide. We opened the first of our Community Guidance Centers for Women at the Rockland County Community College and it offered women individual professional counseling on education, jobs and goals, testing of interests, aptitudes and personal needs, group counseling to explore and deepen personal goals and periodic group guidance courses on paid and unpaid job opportunities, home management, consumer education, community leadership and improved organization of voluntary work.

The State Commerce Department's Women's Program has set up a vocational information project in five community colleges, and the Legislature has provided almost $5 million of state aid for day-care centers as an aid for working mothers, the first such program at the state level since World War II. Our Department of Social Welfare is helping coordinate volunteer work programs, recruitment, training, certification, in hospitals and community service institutions, and our Civil Service Commission has issued a directive for the expanded employment and promotion of women in state government. We have also created the Teachers' Reserve in New York State.

In other words, I am not kidding about this issue—and I do not believe that the Susan B. Anthonys of our generation are kidding either. I am deeply grateful for women's support on conservation, transportation and consumer protection. Women made these programs possible in New York State and are helping to make them work.

I am grateful for women's support of our State Council on the Arts—first in the nation, incidentally—which sponsors about 250 performances each year in more than 100 communities, and makes art exhibitions and other cultural attractions available to millions. And I am grateful for women's support of our recreational programs and acquisitions of scenic land in the Adirondacks and the Hudson Valley.

But my Susan B. Anthony Day thoughts usually revolve less around gratitude than around the hope and the vitality of this national asset that has yet to be truly committed to our national purpose. Who can say what women will accomplish in modern America once they obtain decisive leverage in their fields of special interest, concern and new skills? As Rabbi David J. Seligson of New York City said in an invocation to my conference on women's rights and opportunities:

"We recognize with gratitude the increasing role which

the women of our time are playing in the life of society.

"Theirs is the blessing that rests upon our homes and families.

"Theirs is the life and guidance that molds the souls of the children.

"Theirs also is the right and the eagerness to serve the larger society, to contribute of their wisdom and compassion to the solution of the problems of our time."

VII

FISCAL
INTEGRITY

Before the black-robed graduates under the towering elms of the Old Campus at Yale University, in the spring of 1962, President John F. Kennedy posed the probing questions about the management of our modern economy that unfortunately remain unanswered in our national policy. The fundamental questions were—and still are:

How may our budget and tax policies best be geared to supply adequate revenues and preserve our balance of payments while maintaining and increasing our rate of economic growth?

How may we set our interest rates most wisely, and regulate the flow of money in conjunction with our inde-

pendent financial authorities in ways which will stimu-
late the economy at home without weakening the dollar
abroad?

How can we make our economy work at full capacity,
that is, provide adequate wages for labor and adequate
utilization of plant and opportunity for all, without heading directly for inflation?

Today we have an economic crisis on our hands. The
federal budget is running in excess of $180 billion per
year and the current deficit is estimated in excess of $20
billion. The federal expenditures for the escalated Vietnam war are nearing $35 billion a year. A fragmented,
disorganized war on poverty costs another $28 billion
annually—yet the question of trimming nonessential expenditures and increasing taxes to meet the costs was
evaded in our national policy decisions until inflationary
pressures neared the disaster level. In short, there has been
little evidence of fiscal integrity in Washington. Every
American is hurt by the inflation which results—and the
international portents are ominous indeed.

Fiscal integrity—along with freedom, dignity, opportunity, faith—is of the essence in our federal idea. It implies not revolutionary change in the structure of the
American economy but the balancing of forces and interests with a mutual sense of honor and obligation. This en-
sures to our economy not the bitter class struggles between
good men and bad men that have plagued other countries
and other times but a common search for enlightenment
and the solving of problems.

Our current flight from fiscal integrity is bringing about

our current danger of inflation. The rate of advance in the consumer price index, which had been running at a tolerable 1.2 percent per annum from the end of 1958 through the end of 1965, accelerated to 3 percent in 1967 and more than 4 percent in the spring of 1968. This means that the average worker's take-home pay actually buys less than it did two and a half years ago—the rising prices having eaten away the benefits of dollar gains in wages and salaries. Because inflation bears down with its cruelest weight on low-income and fixed-income families, the federal government may well have done more damage to the well-being of these families through inflation than it has helped them by all the Great Society legislation. And if we permit inflation to develop further, we run the risk of reversion to boom and bust, recession and rising unemployment.

Our flight from fiscal integrity is viewed overseas—by realistic friends as well as subversive foes—as an indication that we are headed for devaluation of the dollar. The foreign run on our gold reserves—in excess of $1 billion a month at its peak—reflects not only speculators' scrambles but the sober assessment of international bankers that we must put our financial house in order or face the traditional penalty. Our federal government has in fact piled up a seemingly endless series of deficits—fifteen in the past seventeen years. On March 15, 1968, American tourists in Western Europe were shocked and stunned when they could not change their dollars at the official rates.

The flight from fiscal integrity may well underlie many of the fears one hears among our people that we cannot possibly cope with all the vast problems we face. It is more than a sense of the size of the problems of the cities, the racial imbalance, health, education, crime in the streets, alienated youth, prevailing violence. It is a suspicion that nothing spent will accomplish much—because the money is being drained away—out of control—to who knows where—and to who knows whom. This is one reason for the anomaly that people are demanding more and more services, but are aggressively uninterested in raising and paying more taxes. Those members of the House of Representatives who declined to approve the Johnson Administration's 10 percent temporary surcharge on income taxes—without a reduction in federal spending of $6 billion per year—were reflecting among other things the public mood about the flight from fiscal integrity.

This situation is even more deplorable when our economy, to judge from its surface sheen of blooming health, has rarely been more prosperous and more productive. The Gross National Product reached the staggering annual rate of $827 billion in the first quarter of 1968—up 7 percent over the first quarter of 1967. In a nation of 200 million people, more than 77 million are at work, and average hourly earnings in manufacturing are approximately $3 per hour, up almost 50 percent in fifteen years. Personal income nationwide is up sharply and if it maintains its present momentum, it should reach $670 billion in 1968—$54 billion more than in 1967. Corporate profits for the first quarter of 1968 amounted to $84.3 billion, or $52.2 billion after taxes. Retail stores sold $27.6 billion worth of goods in a single spring month. Automobile manufacturers, though bothered by the success of foreign imports in holding 10 percent of the market, expect to sell more than eight million cars in America this year, their second best in history. It is quite unacceptable, in the midst of this prosperity, that people should have to ask:

Are the problems too much, the solutions too expensive?

Are the ills so deep that they can be cured only by surgery more drastic than the original ailment?

Are we being asked to do more and mean more at home and abroad than we possibly can?

These questions, these doubts, these fears, these alarms, are inevitable because our federal government has turned its back on fiscal integrity.

Of course we can solve the problems—but first we will have to re-establish fiscal integrity in Washington in order to have the confidence, the sense of purpose, the dedication, the drive we will need. This is not a partisan statement in a Presidential election year. It is an objective statement of fact.

It is a fact that we are by far the strongest and richest nation on earth.

It is a fact that our federal system of government provides institutions at the federal, state and local levels with unique capacity and flexibility to meet our problems.

It is a fact that our private enterprise system has an immense potential for further growth which will, if properly guided and encouraged, allow us to solve our problems in good order.

It is also a fact that the financial needs of our society

preceded and will postdate any termination of the costly conflict in Vietnam—because the financial principles that the federal government has ignored are classical and enduring.

The federal government is overspending and providing inadequate revenue to cover its expenditures. The tragic result is inevitable, at whatever level of expenditure and budgeting, in government and family life alike.

The immediate answers are relatively simple to determine within the framework of fiscal integrity. The federal government must reduce spending and increase taxes. The 10 percent federal income tax surcharge should have been passed two years ago. We must carefully review our commitments around the world to set priorities on what we can and what we cannot do within the limits of our balance of payments situation. We must review, and reduce or postpone federal programs of lower priority to make way for the urgent new attacks we must launch against the problems of poverty and the cities. All these might conceivably reduce the federal deficit from $20 billion plus to a manageable $5 to $8 billion.

None of these moves—these sweeping, decisive, vital moves—will mean a thing—will appear in history as anything more than simple palliatives—forced upon us by pressures we had not foreseen and did not understand—unless we first and foremost, in money matters, comprehend and reflect the role of fiscal integrity in building the greatness of this nation. This requires a basic understanding not only of our history, but of the history of our economy and its governing principles. It is a most exciting story.

In the first place, it was the desire for gold that led Queen Isabella to invest some $60,000 in the voyage of Christopher Columbus in 1492. Even the Puritans, zealous and conscientious as they were in matters of religion, were not immune to the lure of "rewarded hardship" in the New World. The charter of the Massachusetts Bay colony was more concerned with the division of profits from fishing and the fur trade than with Calvinistic theology or equal and just laws. Even when the colonists gave up their dreams of quick riches and settled down to cultivate their new home, they found the going difficult. The travail of Jamestown was to be repeated over and over in other pioneer colonies.

That the colonies did survive and prosper was due to the expansion of commerce between them, as well as between the New and Old Worlds. Tobacco, rice, indigo, furs, dried fish, tar, turpentine, and what we would now call "services" were traded freely amid a ripening fiscal confidence. This sense of stability was fortified by commercial regulation in the colonial governments which, eventually, seeking to ease the risks and the confusions of the money shortage, began to issue their own currency. To avoid being cheated, the colonial traders had to know, for example, that Pennsylvania pounds were solidly backed and sold near par, but that Massachusetts pounds were worth less than 10 percent of their face value in English money.

The whole question of fiscal integrity came to a head

after the Revolutionary War when the colonies, loosely linked under the Articles of Confederation, tried and failed to get trade going again. The central government had no reliable sources of revenue to meet its obligations, foreign trade languished, and trade between the new states was hindered by unreasonable restraints. New Jersey, for example, complained that it was a "cask tapped at both ends" by New York and Pennsylvania. Paper money of all sorts, similar only in worthlessness, clogged the channels of commerce. Continental bonds sold for as little as ten cents on the dollar, giving rise to the expression "not worth a continental," and leading to real doubts about the survival of the new experiment in freedom.

The Constitution of 1787 was, of course, the turning point, designed to bring order into the affairs of men while also upholding their liberty. Two of its provisions were crucial for the commerce of the new nation: 1. states were forbidden to impose tariffs or embargoes on shipments of goods from other states; and 2. the right to issue currency was reserved to the federal government. Both of these provisions were responses to problems which had afflicted the colonies almost from the beginning, and laid the foundation for the economic growth that astonished the world. These "lesser" provisions of the Constitution in fact ranked in importance with those our schoolchildren have learned by heart.

For Secretary of the Treasury, President Washington turned to the brilliant, ambitious Alexander Hamilton, then thirty-two years old. An illegitimate child, born on the West Indies island of Nevis, Hamilton had been educated at Kings College in New York, had written pamphlets against the King, had commanded an artillery company at the age of twenty, and became one of Washington's principal aides. Now he was to build into our destiny as a nation the Hamiltonian fiscal integrity deemed to be fundamental.

Hamilton was our first and greatest Secretary of the Treasury. He first refused to repudiate the national debt of some $56 million, as many of his compatriots urged, and he arranged to take over the unpaid war debts of the states as well, another $18 million. This policy, though denounced because it benefited speculators and propertied men, restored the credit of the nation at one stroke, drew the states together, established the reputation of the United States in world commerce, produced revenue, and provided sound currency for trade.

Hamilton's more controversial Bank of the United States, detested by small farmers in the expanding western and southern states, also proved to have had fiscal merit. President Andrew Jackson, a genuinely anti-business chief executive, destroyed the national bank and deposited federal funds in state banks, known to his enemies as Jackson's "pet banks." These banks issued notes recklessly, money depreciated rapidly, and the Treasury published its famed Specie Circular, announcing that it would accept only metals in payment for public lands. One result was the Panic of 1837 and impoverishment for millions. But in 1846, a truly independent Treasury was created—the government's specie could be maintained in its own values—and fiscal integrity was restored.

The recent history of our economy is more familiar—
yet its story is similarly one of a balance of needs and demands, problems and opportunities, challenges put by
changing technologies and times, in which the indispensable X-factor was confidence.

The Civil War was over, the West was settled, the Industrial Society was burgeoning, the Modern Age was born.
Through the years of expansion, depressions marred the
prospects for many. The Panic of 1873 and the lingering
depression of 1892—which led to the march of Coxey's
army of unemployed on Washington—created a new,
deeper schism between the business world, dominated by
the financial centers of the East, and the agrarians of the
West and South. The schism evolved, in its simplest terms,
into a fight between the interests wedded to gold and the
forces who sought to base the nation's currency on a more
plentiful metal, silver. In 1892, the Populist Party polled
more than a million votes with its cry that "from the same
prolific womb of governmental injustice we breed the two
great classes, tramps and millionaires." Four years later,
William Jennings Bryan captured the Democratic Party
nomination with his famous address: "You shall not press
down upon the brow of labor this crown of thorns, you
shall not crucify mankind upon a cross of gold."

Bryan was unable to win the Presidency, but Theodore
Roosevelt did. We all know how he re-established confi-
dence by re-establishing the balance between "the classes,"
and founding social justice in its modern context. Then
President Woodrow Wilson helped bring into being the
Federal Reserve Board—reflecting his concept that the

nation was suffering under an inflexible credit and currency system with overly centralized control. His Federal Reserve Act provided for a decentralization of the banking system, aiding the West and South, and it gave the federal government increased influence over credit and currency policies. Wilson said that, "Control must be public, not private, must be vested in the government itself, so that the banks may be the instruments, not the masters of business and of individual enterprises and initiative."

The independent Federal Reserve in fact has grown into one of our most cherished bulwarks of fiscal integrity and has developed outstanding leaders such as William McChesney Martin—who has warned for the past several years, I might add, that our federal government is heading for an economic crisis.

The best available estimate of the long-term record of the U.S. economy from 1869 to 1930 was an annual growth of the Gross National Product on the order of 3.75 percent. Then, out of a mare's nest of causes—normalcy, speculation, high tariffs, world unrest, lazy leadership, don't-care public—the Great Depression left its mark on the American dream. There were 12,000,000 unemployed, 32,000 business failures and 5,000 bank failures, and national income fell from $80 billion a year to $40 billion. It was a desperate time and men were willing to listen to desperate proposals, but President Franklin D. Roosevelt made the restoration of confidence his objective. His New Deal measures pumped money into relief and public works programs, into business loans, and banks were reopened—the sound ones—under government insurance to protect depositors against loss. The Securities and Exchange Commission was established to oversee the selling of stocks and bonds. The old gold standard was abandoned. The Wagner Act, the Social Security Act, the Reciprocal Trade Act were passed and millions began to believe, as FDR said, that "the only thing we have to fear is fear itself."

I have always found it interesting, incidentally, that the enduring features of the New Deal had frequently been pretested at the state level—another advantage of our flexible federal system—and that such untested remedies as the NRA, with its familiar Blue Eagle, did not last. But the budget was never balanced—an attempt in 1937 to achieve it was blamed in part for a recession—and the national debt soared ever upward. Only when World War II broke out in Europe did the U.S. economy get rolling again.

Today, I can understand and sympathize with the deeply ingrained fear of massive unemployment that is a heritage among our older people from the Depression. But I am convinced that many of the ideas carried over from this traumatic experience have no real application to the problems we must face in the 1960's and 1970's.

During World War II, our growth rate increased at an average rate of about 10 percent per year. For the postwar period between 1947 and 1960, the annual growth amounted to approximately 4 percent per year.

I believe that vigorous and sustained economic growth is one of our prerequisites. I might add that my associates and I, in New York State, were able to wipe out a potential deficit of $700 million inherited from previous administrations, and to present balanced budgets each year as required by our state laws. On this basis of fiscal integrity, we have proven able to attract $15 billion of new business investment, to increase personal income in the state by 63 percent, and to add 650,000 new jobs to the economy. But despite the growth of the state budget, our total expenditures as a percentage of the personal incomes of our residents are lower than the comparable figures for thirty-six other states. And we rank first among all states in terms of the share of state expenditures paid to localities: 58 percent of the state budget is devoted to aiding local government in the spirit of the federal idea.

New York State taxes—as a percentage of residents' personal incomes—are also lower than those of twenty-six other states.

I am aware of the suspicion that pertains to the spokesman for economic growth—"growthmanship"—and of the pie-in-the-sky labels pinned on to anybody who suggests a 5 percent or 6 percent annual increase in the Gross National Product. Part of this skepticism, I am sure, derives from the excessive hopes attached in the 1960's to "the new economics" with its predictions that rising growth rates would solve all of our problems by magic. The advocates of faster economic growth have often been people who possess no real belief that the institutions of private enterprise can be depended on to produce it. Hence, their advocacy is frequently accompanied by proposals for more and more central planning, implemented by government interventions and controls. These people favor

fiscal and monetary policies, in their essence, that his-
torically have created economic distortion and fed inflation.

I would therefore dissociate myself from those who
argue that massive government spending, creeping inflation and far-reaching government controls provide the
only route toward accelerated economic growth. I am talk-
ing about growth that is obtainable within the terms of
reference of our proven system. I believe we can grow
faster and do so without inflation and without a spreading
network of government controls. I have full confidence
that America has the ability to achieve the goals it pur-
sues. I have full confidence that America has the resolution to support the policies and make the hard choices
essential for solving our problems and achieving more
rapid economic progress.

Bottomed on fiscal integrity, the economic growth rate
of our country is of fundamental import. If it is assumed
that our long-term growth rate is something like a dou-
bling every twenty-five years, then it also follows that
minimal percentage point changes applied to an $827 bil-
lion Gross National Product amount to really huge sums.
Without an increase in tax rates, without an increase in
the average growth rate, federal tax revenues increase by
an average of at least $10 billion per year. These revenues
went up $43 billion between fiscal 1964 and fiscal 1968
despite the tax cut of 1964. This is what I might term our
fiscal dividend, or growth bonus. But if we increase federal government spending more than the fiscal dividend
permits, in flourishing business conditions, and if we do

not increase revenues by increasing taxes, the sure result will be inflation. This is what we have today.

We have the potential, in my judgment, to expand the real output of the U.S. economy by at least 4½ percent per year and quite possibly by more. This would increase our total production by at least 19 percent in four years, 25 percent in five years, and 55 percent in ten years.

Consider, for example, these factors:

· U.S. investment in education, which plays a crucial role in economic expansion, is now almost $50 billion a year and is growing at 10 percent per year.

· U.S. research and development has assumed an entirely new dimension, with spending in 1968 reaching $25 billion, or four times the 1955 total. Because of the time lags involved, we are just beginning to reap the benefits of this and may well be on the threshold of further astonishing advances in technology and creation of whole new industries.

· The revolution in management techniques and training—and retraining—now under way will contribute to growth and to a still higher motivation and productivity of working men and women.

· Our economy generates huge savings for investment: this year we shall invest some $120 billion, an amount greater than the Gross National Product of the United Kingdom or West Germany or Japan. These investments will support and power further growth.

In terms of current dollars, our Gross National Product might be expected to exceed $1 trillion by 1972 and more than $1.5 trillion by 1978. With such a rate of growth,

U.S. families will be able to raise their real standard of living by 2½ percent to 3 percent per year, by some 10 percent to 12½ percent by 1972 and about one-third by 1978, which is very high. By 1978, more than 70 percent of all families would have incomes with a real purchasing power of $6,000 or more as against half of that today. Half of all families would have incomes of $10,000 or more— more than double today's level. This increase might be expected to bring millions of families up from below the present poverty line.

It is, therefore, vital to our whole national life that we restore balance to our fiscal affairs. It is necessary to discipline ourselves to set clear priorities and to make hard choices. And these choices will demand rare political courage. For they will determine what things we shall immediately do and what things we shall—reluctantly but responsibly—defer. This is not to give higher place or fuller attention to the crisis of our dollar than to the crisis of our society. Rather it is to say that only a sound, healthy, dynamic economy will permit us to mobilize the vast and expanding resources we need to rebuild our cities, to erase poverty, and to heal our society.

The exciting truth is that a more full and more rewarding and more meaningful life for all Americans lies directly ahead—if only our leadership applies reason and prudence in our economic affairs, if only Alexander Hamilton's example of fiscal integrity and the lessons of our economic history as a nation are heeded and applied.

VIII

THE
OTHER WORLD

We begin by invading the house to strip it of its furniture. Everything goes: bed, chairs, tables, television set. We will leave the family with a few old blankets, a kitchen table, a wooden chair. . . . The box of matches may stay, a small bag of flour, some sugar and salt. A few moldy potatoes already in the garbage can must be rescued, for they will provide much of tonight's meal.

The bathroom is dismantled, the running water shut off, the electric wires taken out. Next, we take away the house. The family can move to the toolshed. Communications must go next. No more newspapers, magazines, books. . . . Next, government services must go. No more mailmen, no more firemen. There is a school, but it is three miles away and consists of two rooms. They are not too overcrowded since only half the children in the neighborhood go to school.

The nearest clinic is ten miles away and is tended by a midwife. It can be reached by bicycle provided the family has a bicycle, which is unlikely.

Finally, money. We will allow our family a cash hoard of five dollars.

This process of reduction of an American family to the living standards of most of the people in the world, described by Robert L. Heilbroner in *The Great Ascent,* is perhaps the beginning of a calm, unsentimental understanding of the second greatest crisis we face—the greatest being the maintenance of Churchill's apocalyptic nuclear stalemate—"in which safety will be the sturdy child of terror, and survival the twin brother of annihilation."

The dimensions of the crisis of the other world—most of Asia, Africa, the Middle East and Latin America—are absolutely fundamental. First, between 1965 and 1985 the number of human beings on our planet will increase from 3.3 billion at least to 5 billion. In the following fifteen years, the total world population, if the growth is not checked, will increase to 7.15 billion. Within the next forty years, there will be more than twice as many people as there are right now. Second, the population of the other world is augmenting at an infinitely faster pace than that of our world. In 1900, the peoples of the less-developed regions comprised 67 percent of the world's total, in 1960 about 70 percent, and by A.D. 2000 the other world will have almost 80 percent of the population.

As Adlai Stevenson pointed out:

"There is in the moiling masses of Asia a tremendous power, potentially the greatest power on earth, and today our enemies conspire to gain the mastery of this power. They have at their disposal, as we all know, a powerful weapon, for Communism is a perversion of the dream of justice. And while we see its leading attribute as the perversion, the illiterate, the toiling masses, still have their eyes fixed on the dream.

"We too have a powerful weapon, truth, and we gain our strength from our thoughtful citizenry, which seeks and holds the truth with both its heart and its mind. The question is, however, whether we have come to decisive responsibility too early, before we were ready, before we had matured sufficiently. No man can say with certainty. Personally, I am optimistic and confident, but this question will not be answered tomorrow. It will be answered in *your* lifetime, and it will be answered in large part by *you*, the privileged American."

Ten thousand men, women and children die every day in the other world from starvation, malnutrition or directly associated causes. One and a half billion of the other world's people are malnourished and seven out of ten of all the children subsist on a critically inadequate diet. Food production is catastrophically out of balance. The less developed areas, with some 70 percent of the people, produce 47 percent of our grains on an average 0.43 acres of land per capita, while the advanced nations, only fractionally as large in land surface and with 30 percent of the world's people, produce 53 percent of the grain on 0.85 acres of land per capita. Despite all the progress in science and technology of the past 150 years, there are more hungry people, and a higher proportion of hungry people, than in Queen Victoria's world.

The population explosion aggravates the food shortage to the edge of total intolerability. The chief of the Perspective Planning Division of the Indian Government's

Planning Commission, says that: "To increase consumption of food grain in India by two ounces per head . . . will require an increase of nine million tons in annual supplies. This means an increase of more than 10 percent in domestic production or, alternatively, an increase in export expenditures of $750 millions, which is more than half of India's total export earnings." Here we see another element of the dreadful pressures: the underdeveloped countries have no money, or very little, to contribute to their own nutrition. So, as Dr. Earl Butz, Dean of Agriculture at Purdue University, summed up, "The world is on a collision course. When the massive force of an exploding population meets the much more stable line of world food production, something must give."

Forbes magazine adds this plain talk:

"The malnourished masses love their children as intensely as well-fed Americans love theirs. They are not about to starve peacefully and quietly, in patience, resignation and fatalism, as their ancestors might have done. They know there is a world without hunger somewhere outside their dusty villages. They have transistor radios, and they have bumped in rickety buses into market towns. They have taken seriously the politicians' promises of a better life. They will riot and kill to achieve it. They are doing so right now."

Dr. Raymond Ewell, of the New York State University, said that if present trends of population growth and food production continue, famine will reach serious proportions in India, Pakistan and China in the early 1970's, and in

Indonesia, Iran, Turkey, Egypt and Brazil, among other countries, in the next decade. This, he adds, will be "the most colossal catastrophe in history."

Lammot Du Pont Copeland, chairman of the board of E. I. du Pont de Nemours & Company, says that, "In the very abundance of swelling human numbers, the poverty of most of mankind is rooted. This truth, in the short arc of a dozen years, has etched itself deeply into the minds of scholars and physicians, priests and presidents, leaders of industry and science. I confess, like many others, I once took for granted the notion that a rapidly growing population almost automatically meant rising profits and better life for more people. I have learned that for the world as a whole, this is not so. And for America, it will not be so much longer."

The Kaiser Aluminum & Chemical Corporation, in its booklet *The Promised Land*, concludes that, "Perhaps, in the end, what we have to offer that other world is not so much a political system, or even individual freedom, but simply how to increase the abundance of material things so that a man can think more about what he believes in than he does about his belly. And then, it may be that he will choose freedom—as once, given the same choice, we did."

I have drawn upon the counsel of so many authorities on this problem because it is our first order of business, in my opinion, to define the gravity of the situation. It is *the* problem that defies facile solution. Its size is monumental: India's population, for example, has *grown* since 1966 by the equivalent of the entire population of both North and South Vietnam, in which we are engaged in a $35 billion-a-year war without result.

Between our world and the other world, there is no common heritage, no pervasive friendship or hatred, only a relationship of civilizations brushing into one another and bruising one another, on balance, indecisively. There are few common institutions, few channels of contact—and one of our classic original errors in planning our foreign aid programs in Asia and Africa, at least, was to assume that they would succeed "like the Marshall Plan." In ravaged Europe, of course, the problem was to restore democratic institutions and revive the condition, morale and energies of the people. In the other world, there is no restoration, no revival, no reach, in the context of the U.S.-European partnership that made the Marshall Plan the landmark of the mid-century. The less developed nations have little experience, skilled manpower or institutions of self-government upon which they can rely.

The national questioning of whether foreign aid to the other world was, in fact, feasible or realistic, has reflected itself most dramatically in terms of the amount of money spent. U.S. aid on the world scene took on its economic development format—as distinct from political "dollar diplomacy"—quite recently. Congress had voted in 1812 to send grain to Venezuela after an earthquake there; it authorized Navy shipping to transport relief supplies to Ireland in 1847 and 1880, and sent one of the first government-financed technical assistance missions to Liberia in

1909. But all this did not get into big money until World War I. Then the U.S. war loans and aid to the Allies netted us a $7 billion loss, followed by an additional $3.1 billion in post-Armistice loans for relief and reconstruction. U.S. assistance in World War II was a staggering $40.93 billion—and during the first sixteen years after the war, U.S. aid to some 100 countries has been reckoned at almost $56 billion more. But here, however, are the spending trends of the 1960's:

· U.S. commitments of economic assistance averaged $2.5 billion per year in the late 1950's and increased to an average $4 billion per year in the period 1960–65 but the rising trend was stabilized in 1962;

· U.S. military aid to less-developed countries, which affects the performance of their economies as well as their military security, has averaged $1.3 billion per year;

· U.S. allies have contributed far more than is generally realized in this country to the foreign aid effort—the U.S. in fact has provided only 58 percent of free, developed countries' aid to the other world since 1956—and Western European countries tend to concentrate their aid in former colonial regions.

· The U.S. has consistently hardened its terms of assistance in recent years, with aid increasingly tied to procurement in the U.S.; loans rose from 42 percent to 60 percent of "bilateral commitments" in the 1960's and loans increasingly became repayable in dollars, at higher rates of interest.

Professor John D. Montgomery of Harvard University,

chairman of the Committee on International Development Research of the Society for International Development, comments on the trend: "Foreign aid has always suffered from an irresistible popular tendency to pull up the plant to see if its roots are still growing. Despite this, foreign aid has survived. . . . [But] the laurels bestowed on the United States a decade ago for excellence in foreign aid had worn somewhat thin by the mid-1960's. Whereas the 1949 aid appropriation was 11.5 percent of the federal budget, the 1965 appropriation was less than 4 percent—less because of dissatisfaction with results than out of indifference, disillusion and even despair." *Business Week* magazine wrote in the winter of 1968:

RICH COUNTRIES GET RICHER . . . BUT
THEY KEEP LID ON AID TO POOR NATIONS

This meant that the fifteen industrial nations are devoting a decreasing percentage of their increasing Gross National Products to foreign aid to the other world. The so-called "development gap" is widening.

There are countless organizations in the field, among them the World Bank with $22.8 billion in capital subscribed by 106 member nations and $11 billion in loans to date; the United Nations, especially its Food and Agricultural Organization, with 2,000 employees in its Rome headquarters and another 2,600 in the field; the U.S. labor movement, under the leadership of the development-minded president of the A.F.L.-C.I.O., George Meany; U.S. universities and European universities with partnership projects with their counterparts in the other world;

U.S. philanthropic foundations with their specialized knowledge and experience of medical, agricultural and demographic operations; the U.S. armed forces which, in their deployment for our national security, assume many pacification roles out of war zones; and the Peace Corps— "perhaps it will be for the generation of the Peace Corps," says Professor Montgomery, "to supply the mixture of imagination and patience required to fulfill the promise of an enlightened and effective foreign aid program in the twentieth century."

The basic fact of the matter is, however, that the problem of the other world is growing at a rate inestimably greater than our efforts to cope with it. It is just as true today, as I remarked in 1963, that our country cannot carry on a unilateral basis the economies of fifty, sixty or a hundred nations. It is harder now than then for the U.S. to commit massive funds to the underdeveloped countries in view of our massive new needs for our own war against poverty—in view of our balance of payments difficulties— in view of our inability, to date, to set realistic priorities and define meaningful targets.

What then may we do, and how ought we to order our effort? In his original Point Four statement, President Truman defined the basic objectives.

"We must embark on a bold new program for making the benefits of our scientific advance and industrial progress available for the improvement and growth of underdeveloped areas. . . . For the first time in history, humanity possesses the knowledge and skill to relieve the sufferings of these people."

Now, we ought to redefine and reorganize our foreign aid in terms of clear and consistent *principles*.

I will italicize the words I believe to be applicable in a passage from *The Diplomacy of Economic Development,* by the former head of the World Bank, Eugene R. Black, a definitive book on the subject:

"The plain fact is that the conditions for a full integration of the political and economic aims of the rich and the poor nations in the free world community do not exist, nor is it possible to foresee a time in the future when they will.

"For the rich nations, the problem is *to live constructively with* the historic transformation going on in the underdeveloped world, *not to try to solve it.*

"The values of freedom and democracy cannot be sold like soap; nor are they the necessary result of economic development.

"People in the West came to respect these values *only gradually over many years.*

"If respect for them is to spread among the people of the underdeveloped world, the West must be willing to *work side by side with* these people and *make common cause with* them.

"For it is not by any sudden act of conversion, but only through *growing together over time* that the West can hope its values will take root and spread.

"This growing together will take *constant and constructive contact*—and *that is what* the exercise of *economic aid*—or development diplomacy, as I have called it —*is all about.*"

Second, we ought to set very clear *priorities*—and in

many instances in the other world the priority has to be to head off the collision of which I have spoken between the population and the food production statistics. This is no vague generality: it implies the downgrading of the industrialization schemes cherished by most of the new nations. This means, to stress it, that our aid to the other world ought to be zeroed in on the food production and population problems.

Third, we must continue to enlist the support of our allies for the building of new nations, viable political institutions and a higher quality of life in the other world.

Fourth, we must enlist the aid of experts in the field and heed the advice of Eugene Black in our recruitment and training of professionals in the underdeveloped countries. We need to emphasize the development of the *human resources* of the other world.

Fifth, we must clarify our principles within our new priorities. An example of what I mean is a statement made by Dr. J. George Harrar, president of the Rockefeller Foundation, before the House Committee on Agriculture in Washington. Dr. Harrar said:

"It is a humanitarian proposition to suggest that the more advanced and affluent countries of the world should assume the burden of feeding the hungry nations through intensive agricultural overproduction to produce surpluses. But taken alone, this course would place a continuing and growing burden on all of the producer nations involved and could at best be only a short-term expedient, as well as a force disruptive to the local economy. A more rational approach would be a large-scale and well-organized effort toward overcoming the tremendous underproduction which plagues so much of the world today.

"Thus, donations of surplus foods—and occasionally even of some that are not surplus—may be necessary to prevent calamities such as famine, disease and strife. Ultimately, however, this process, if unaccompanied by self-help, can result only in a trend toward a common economic denominator detrimental to all concerned.

"The only workable plan requires the mobilization of knowledge, methods, materials and technology in a consortium of effort to bring about improvements in all aspects of agricultural technology in those nations whose production figures are substantially lower than their potentials."

Dr. Harrar is in fact a professional agronomist who has succeeded by setting principles within priorities. He was instrumental as the leader of a Rockefeller Foundation task force, working under the direction of the Mexican government and in cooperation with Mexican agricultural experts, which proved able to increase Mexico's production of wheat and corn in the 1940's and 1950's. Twenty years ago, Mexico's then population of 21 million received an average 1,700 calories of food per day, while today's 37 million Mexicans receive 2,700 calories per person per day—and the country became self-sufficient in wheat in 1956, corn in 1958. Tough and durable Mexican "dwarf wheat" was brought to India at the end of 1963 and, after field testing, was distributed throughout the country, yielding up to 50 percent more than the local varieties. Then Dr. D. S. Athwal, of Punjab Agricultural University, an authority in cross-breeding and hybridization, continued to experiment with thousands of other Mexican breeding lines and produced another dwarf wheat that averaged 30 percent greater yield than the original import from Mexico. He has since discovered other promising dwarfs—and the next problem is to broaden distribution.

This is no gobbledygook—it is the language of the just war of national liberation for the millions of the other world—and it is infinitely more meaningful than discourses by healthy, happy Westerners about the meaning of freedom and democracy, at least until the other world is healthier and happier.

The Ford Foundation, in much the same kind of professional spirit, has had similarly encouraging results with rice production, working with Indian agronomists in Tanjore. This is another specific crisis of the other world: though India contains a third of the world's area under rice production, and produces 31 percent of the world's rice output, its average yield per acre is depressingly small, only 600 pounds per acre compared to 2,250 for Japan, 3,100 for Italy and 3,230 for Spain—a difference not entirely accounted for by primitive agricultural methods. With vital assistance from favorable monsoon rains, with booming production of the new rice seeds, an Indian project director in Tanjore said that, "Tradition does not stand in our way here. The difficulty now is providing enough seed and fertilizer for the farmers who want it."

In fact, India's recent agricultural gains tell a remarkable and promising story of rejuvenation in the other world today—and indicate that the problems *may* be soluble.

When developing nations are determined and eager to modernize their agriculture—and to devote their own priority to this in their own national planning—their friends with greater resources may help them to work out realistic plans which will 1. bring about required adjustments in agricultural production patterns and, 2. lead to increased average yield and higher-quality farm products. Successful agricultural technology today is no mystery and, using available information and available assistance, developing nations may do much to help themselves. Some important steps include:

· Emphasis on and reinforcement of agricultural research, education and extension, staffed by qualified specialists to keep farmers currently and constantly informed on their profession;

· Provision of adequately supervised credit—exorbitantly expensive everywhere in the underdeveloped countries, if available at all—thus permitting improved management and the abolition, eventually, of subsistence agriculture, and the provision of incentives and personal rewards;

· Development of an agricultural support mechanism ranging from transportation to marketing facilities that are often almost nonexistent;

· Drastic expansion of the domestic production—with foreign capital, if necessary—and import of inorganic fertilizers and herbicides, pesticides and fungicides—and augmented sales, subsidies and gifts to farmers of cheap fertilizers of all descriptions.

Success is predicated upon a series of small victories

which together are synergistic, it has been well said, and if, simultaneously, significant progress is made toward stabilization of populations, then the future will be brighter. This means the population planners, along with the agronomists, are among the key people within the priorities of our "just wars of national liberation" in the other world.

The United States cannot thrive over the long run unless conditions of stability, security and prosperity prevail—eventually—in the increasingly interdependent world. For these reasons, along with our traditional commitment to humanitarian principles, it is in our self-interest to help narrow the development gap. And we should be looking more for steady and sustained improvement rather than for dramatic, short-term effects. We should approach the problem of aiding nations in terms of mutually agreed criteria directed at real progress rather than in terms of competition in the Cold War. It follows that our assistance must not be pre-emptive: we must make it clear that we are neither to offer a crutch, nor wield a whip. Feasible reforms should be encouraged—but we should not attempt to impose arbitrary standards from the outside.

In addition to the educational and political contributions we may be able to make, we should pay attention in many instances to the problem of how best to help the underdeveloped nations service the debts incurred in previous aid programs. This should be done on a cooperative basis with other industrial loaning nations if possible.

I would add that there is, obviously, a vast opportunity and a vast risk for private enterprise in this field. Arthur

K. Watson, chairman of the IBM World Trade Corp., heading a committee of businessmen, educators, labor leaders and government officials on the problem, reported that more than $13 billion of U.S. private investments had been located in underdeveloped countries until 1964—and this figure is much greater today. American businessmen were used to taking risks, said Watson, but not many were accustomed to accepting "political instability, threats and rumors of expropriation, systems of pervasive discretionary regulation, prospects of rapid inflation and devaluation, and other novel features of overseas investment."

My point in discussing these technicalities of foreign aid —rather than the usual generalized concepts—is that therein lies the best hope of coping with some of the problems of the other world by specific and realistic action. As Eugene Black wrote in *The Diplomacy of Economic Development*, and again I italicize:

"Piecing these fragmentary observations together, one gets the picture of a field strewn with obstacles, some of which are immovable and others of which can be pushed aside. So far as it goes, this is not an inaccurate picture, but it is not complete: it lacks a dynamic element.

"In reality, the obstacles in the path of development are changing form and character all the time because, *in reality, economic development and social change are interacting all the time.*

"In the underdeveloped world, today, society is continually adapting itself to make use of existing knowledge.

Development is proceeding in spite of the cultural attitudes, social institutions and political conflicts which sometimes seem to be immovable barriers.

"It is not a smooth, uninterrupted progression, to be sure; rather, *growth appears more as a series of fits and starts.*

"And yet, as Galileo is supposed to have said, it moves."

In my own professional lifetime, I have been an agricultural developer in Venezuela and Brazil, a foreign aid administrator in Washington, and a committee planner of the International Finance Corporation and the International Development Association. If I have learned anything from these facets of my experience, it is to move and to plan very precisely—to integrate all of the factors of the whole and not deal merely in fragments. As I said once in South America after an embarrassing non-success:

"We made mistakes, some of them big mistakes. We also had administrative troubles. Some of our people were not familiar with local conditions. There were some language problems. We had some incompetents and had to make costly changes in management. We didn't have enough experience—nobody had had much experience in this kind of pioneering work—and that includes me. We were constantly improvising to overcome unexpected obstacles and at times we floundered in the field. But we learned, and the most important thing we learned was not to try to start on too big a scale. We thought we had reasons for starting out big in various projects, but it was a mistake and we should have known it.

"For example: take our efforts to mechanize tropical agriculture. We went in thinking we could slay the dragon by introducing modern machinery, and we flopped. We didn't know enough then to do the job. What was needed was experimental work."

We *can* do something about the staggering problems that other world poses—but experience tells us to proceed with caution.

IX

UNITY
IN THE WEST

The federal idea, which our Founding Fathers applied in their historic act of political creation in the eighteenth century, can be applied in this twentieth century in the larger context of the world of free nations—if we will but match our forefathers in courage and vision. The first historic instance secured freedom and order to this new nation. The second can decisively serve to guard freedom and promote order in a free world. Sweeping as this assertion may be, I believe it to be anything but an academic proposition. Quite the contrary, it is a matter of cold political realism.

My concern is therefore less with the specific manifestations of disunity—worrisome though these are—between the United States on the one hand and our closest friends of the North Atlantic Treaty Organization on the other hand. In the inevitable and continuing readjustment of relationships between us—sharpened and aggravated by our virtually unilateral commitment in Vietnam—a measure of disagreement and hostility among friends is not surprising. There have been political, personal and psychological clashes which have been accentuated on both sides by an overconcern with tactics and a tendency to treat the symptoms and overlook the causes of what has been going wrong. Instead, we need to remember that the genius of the federal idea is that it promotes diversity within unity and is, as such, transferable. George Washington, after the ratification of the Constitution, wrote to his former subordinate commander Lafayette:

"We have sowed the seeds of liberty and union that will spring up everywhere on earth. Some day, taking the pattern from the United States, there will be founded a United States of Europe."

Not long ago, the new chief executive of the Common Market, Jean Rey, pointed to a bound copy of *The Federalist* in his office in Brussels and said, "We are in the same process that you Americans went through 200 years ago. We may have our quarrels between federalists and nationalists, but everyone knows very well we are moving toward unity."

It is a basic fact that no nation in today's world can be an island or a fortress unto itself. Not safety alone, but survival in the nuclear balance, depends for any nation upon the effective guarding of all. This kind of unity, however, demands much more than defensive attitudes and hopes. In the deeper sense, only common, creative political purpose—a true and binding dedication to serve the aspirations of all men for the betterment of their lives —can seal nations in lasting compact. And it is only through a shared sense of affirmative purpose that free nations can achieve their purposes.

True cooperation demands not merely exhortation but explicit understandings, among them:

1. There must be shared values and goals—a comparable comprehension of the nature of man and his place in the universe, specifically with reference to freedom, justice, opportunity, dignity and the rule of law;

2. There must be a sustained reflection on the part of the partners in their national conduct that each respects the good—and the need—of all.

3. These values and these policies must be codified in the form of shared institutions that are, in fact, going concerns, and are recognized and upheld by the peoples of the various partners.

The greatness of the North Atlantic community is that it meets the tests of all of these three imperatives. We do hold comparable values. We do consider one another in the preparation of our policies. We have begun to develop joint organizations that lend force and substance to our intent. As such, although the military side of NATO is under erosion, although Vietnam has shaken confidence, although there is a new and dangerous American isolationism in the air, I believe we are in these regions of the world building on a measure of strength. I believe we may move on toward new concepts of regional groupings. These will bring our struggle for unity into a wholly new dimension.

My first involvement with regional policy planning began in the autumn of 1944, when I was appointed Assistant Secretary of State in charge of Latin American Affairs in President Franklin D. Roosevelt's Administration. Then the crisis was Argentina, in the midst of World War II, and the storm center was the dictator, Juan Perón. The United States had asked all Latin American countries to withdraw recognition of Argentina, but four had refused, and the United States had declined to consider joint action with other republics to deal with the situation. Meanwhile, the United States and its major allies in World War II had not consulted with the Latin American countries about their postwar plans for a United Nations—and many feared that cooperation within the hemisphere was a casualty. At the suggestion of an old friend, Rafael Oreamuno, formerly minister from Costa Rica, I invited three Latin American ambassadors to lunch, and I was assured that the neighbors of Argentina were simply afraid to denounce Perón. Then the conversation turned to the possibility of regional action—by *all* of the South American countries—to protect any single country that was attacked. "The key to the solution," said one ambassador, would be "an inter-American basis for solving problems of peace and security as well as economic problems."

Twice in January of 1945, in company with Secretary of State Edward R. Stettinius, I conferred about the problem with President Roosevelt. My point was that the Latin American countries were concerned about Big Power domination of the United Nations but that, in a coming foreign ministers' conference in Mexico City, they would support United Nations principles—provided that the United States would help develop and strengthen a regional inter-American system. This was a hot issue in the State Department. There the International Division feared that such a regional grouping might damage the prospects of the world organization. Roosevelt supported me and, when pressed by the International Division, I was able to say, "My instructions come from the President. If you want to change this policy, you will have to take it up with him."

The Inter-American Conference on Problems of War and Peace, as the Mexico City meeting was called, was historic in the sense that it led to the Act of Chapultepec. This provided for nothing less than a mutual guarantee of all the boundaries of all the Latin American republics against aggression from any source. An attack against an American republic would be an attack against all, the Act of Chapultepec said, and would,be resisted by all. Two months later, Argentina itself signed the Act and agreed to abide by it and, by declaring war against the Axis Powers, obtained a U.S. commitment to move for Argentina's admission to the United Nations. Early in April, 1945, Franklin D. Roosevelt died.

On the eve of the U.N.'s founding conference at San Francisco, there formed within the State Department, on the Argentina-U.N. issue, a rare coalition of "liberal" and "conservative" factions. The "liberals" were against U.N. membership for Argentina on principle, and the "conservatives" were resentful of Perón for his on-again, off-again support of the Axis Powers throughout the war.

Secretary Stettinius told me: "In view of the unhappy feelings between you and members of the International Division, I believe it would be best if you did not go to San Francisco. You had full freedom in Mexico City and now they want the same freedom at San Francisco."

But within a few hours, Stettinius changed his mind: the Latin American countries, fearful that their interests would be sacrificed at the U.N., concerned that the Act of Chapultepec would be outlawed under the new charter, were indicating that they might not follow the American lead at San Francisco. Because the votes of the Latin American republics would be needed in the event of a showdown with the Russians, Stettinius overruled Leo Pasvolsky and Alger Hiss, of the International Division, and told me to go to San Francisco for "a few days—just to get things started." Off I went with a planeload of Latin American delegates. I was to stay there for the duration of the conference—and was to live through one of the stirring struggles of our times. This began almost at once when Soviet Foreign Minister Vyacheslav Molotov launched an open tirade against Mexico's Foreign Minister Padilla, charging that he was an American puppet, and against all Latin American traditions in general.

The Latin American delegates felt strongly that the United States should honor its commitment to support the invitation of Argentina and Secretary Stettinius ruled in their favor. After seemingly interminable chessboard maneuvers with the Russians, Argentina was admitted, in plenary session, by 32 votes to 4, with a dozen or so abstentions. Then there was a new threat: the United States had agreed tentatively to an amendment to the United Nations Charter which would permit the Russians to form "regional arrangements" in Europe and Asia while yet being permitted to veto such other types of mutual security pacts as the Act of Chapultepec.

"Therefore," as an American delegate, Senator Arthur Vandenberg of Michigan, wrote in his diary, "in the event of trouble in the Americas, we could not act ourselves; we would have to depend exclusively on the Security Council; and any one permanent member of the Council could veto the latter action (putting us at the mercy of Britain, Russia or China). Thus, little is left of the Monroe Doctrine." Our approval of this amendment had been taken against my opposition, and so I asked for an appointment with Secretary Stettinius, only to be told that he was not seeing anybody that weekend due to fatigue, and I should discuss the matter with Assistant Secretary James C. Dunn or Leo Pasvolsky.

Feelings by this time had been running pretty high—I had been accused of being "anti-Russian" and "pro-Fascist," and the Latin Americans had been similarly slandered in the press. I therefore decided not to see Dunn and Pasvolsky but Senator Vandenberg, instead. At dinner, I told him that the Latin American republics were shocked at the proposed amendment and were convinced that the Act of Chapultepec was in danger. I also confided to him some of my own views on the situation. Vandenberg decided that the solution was to add a sentence to the proposed amendment that would exempt Chapultepec from the veto power and he began to draft a letter to Stettinius. The Colombian foreign minister, Lleras Camargo, and the Cuban ambassador, Guillermo Belt, came over and approved the letter. The toughest part of it was a warning by Vandenberg that the U.S. Senate might not approve the U.N. charter if the Monroe Doctrine was infringed.

The Vandenberg letter caused an explosion in the U.S. delegation. As Joe Alex Morris has written, "The fact that the Assistant Secretary of State in charge of Latin American Affairs previously had been opposing the amendment was one thing. Rockefeller could be brushed off. But the fact that a powerful member of the United States Senate had been brought into the controversy was quite another thing and could not be brushed off, especially since Senator Tom Connally lined up with Vandenberg's position." And, as Vandenberg wrote in his diary:

"I served notice on the Delegation, as a matter of good faith, that if this question is not specifically cleared up in the Charter, I shall expect to see a reservation on the subject in the Senate, and that I shall support it. . . . At the end of an acrimonious session . . . the subject was temporarily referred to a special committee of technicians."

Meanwhile, the Latin American delegates met with Stettinius and convinced him of their sincerity in holding out for their mutual security arrangements, veto-free. Foreign policy adviser Harold Stassen drafted a memorandum suggesting language for the amendment that would recognize the inherent right of self-defense, along with the one-for-all, all-for-one concept of Chapultepec. Vandenberg wrote a substitute amendment that said, "In the application of this provision, the principles of the Act of Chapultepec and of the Monroe Doctrine are specifically recognized." The British and other delegations, concerned that the Russians might wreck the whole conference, balked, but only at inclusion of Chapultepec's name.

On June 9, 1945, Article 51 of the United Nations Charter, unanimously approved by the conference, stated that no provision of the Charter "shall impair the inherent right of individual or collective self-defense if an armed attack occurs against a member of the United Nations." Subsequent clauses of the Charter authorized pacts "appropriate to regional action."

In the perspective of history, this was a critical victory. We had won our Act of Chapultepec. We had also, in Article 51, laid the basis for the foundation of the North Atlantic Treaty Organization four years later. It is also on the record that, at a formal dinner not long after the NATO signing, I found myself seated next to John Foster Dulles, who had served as a Republican foreign policy adviser at the San Francisco Conference. "I owe you an apology, Nelson," Dulles said. "If you fellows hadn't done it, we might never have had NATO."

The North Atlantic Treaty Organization—the regional grouping—provided the security in which the Marshall Plan went to work, Western Europe prospered, Marxist economic illusions withered, and the European Economic

Community, the Common Market, forged a mighty trading bloc of more than 175 million people. These were—and are—even though slowly—leading toward the United States of Europe of which George Washington spoke. Across lowered tariff fences, goods spilled into markets where previously they had been rare and expensive. French women shopped for Italian shoes, German appliances and Dutch pottery, while West German housewives bought French cognac and Belgian vegetables, and Dutch businessmen drove to work in Fiats or Renaults. In Milan, workers took their evening meals out of German refrigerators, ate them off Dutch china, settled back in front of their Belgian TV sets to watch an Italy vs. France soccer game on Eurovision, the continent-wide television network.

In the cycle of rising output, rising incomes and rising demand, Common Market industrial production soared an amazing 12 percent in 1960 alone, compared to 4.5 percent for the United States. Between 1950 and 1960, steel production in the European Economic Community rose by 75 percent. Unemployment all but vanished and, until the boom leveled off recently, jobs were filled by scores of thousands of migrant workers. On vacation, Western Europeans drove, cycled, flew or traveled by train across borders behind which armies had once massed, and fraternized freely, if sometimes skeptically, with one another.

But if the Western Europeans were rejoicing in the economic fruits of the new unity, they were probably just as aware of the political problems and implications. To Americans flying across Europe by jet, it was hard to understand how so many people crowded into such a small land-space had so many different languages, customs and traditions. To the Western Europeans, the land itself bore the mark of past disunity and suspicions. That field might be Agincourt, where English longbowmen broke the charge of the French cavalry, and that village might be Waterloo. The town over there was perhaps Verdun, or Sedan, or Solferino, or Bastogne in the Battle of the Bulge. Only in the shadow of the hydrogen bomb and under the protection of NATO were the dreamers of Western union accepted as realists. And as production sent prosperity and confidence soaring, some Western Europeans began to talk in terms of a new world power, a third force between, as a facetious European put it, *les barbares primitifs*, the Russians, and *les barbares civilisés*, the United States.

The new danger was that Western Europe, in consolidating its own unity, was contributing to a new world disunity. The danger reached for reality when France vetoed Great Britain's application for membership in the Common Market even though West Germany, Italy and the Benelux countries wanted her in. Meanwhile, the Soviet military threat was construed by most Western Europeans to have lessened, and dependence upon the U.S. deterrent shrank. The Eastern European countries made tentative, then dramatic, moves to ease themselves out of the Soviet grip. There was clearly a new ferment.

Meanwhile, our own relations with the NATO countries

tended to grow sterile. We must re-establish with our friends an atmosphere of candor, trust, confidence and cooperation. We must consult. We must offer a call and a challenge more clearly positive than shrill cries of anti-Communism. In the last analysis, our power as well as our prestige in the world depend upon our commitment to progress and freedom. We should, specifically, as we face Western Europe, take heed of its renewed sense of integrity and independence. We must stress its own responsibility. This demands of us new perceptions of its changed economic, military and political circumstances. For these open up unique opportunities for new—and unifying—political relationships. And we must never lose our sense of perspective when things do not always go the way we believe they should.

The North Atlantic alliance remains the strongest, closest, most successful peacetime association ever formed among free nations. Europe's nationalism has revived strongly enough to reject a series of U.S.-sponsored schemes for military integration and moves toward explicitly supranational political organs such as a European parliament have ground to a halt. Europe's reviving nationalism is also a significant factor in the steep decline of an extranational ideology, Communism, in Western Europe. Yet few in Europe today believe that the integrationist trend represented by the Common Market and the looser European Free Trade Association will be reversed.

"In short," *Fortune* magazine sums up, "Western Europe

refused to choose between nationalism and integration. It chose both."

Jean Monnet, co-founder and first president of the European Coal and Steel Community in 1950, prophet of European Union ever since, adds that, "Just as the United States found it necessary to unite, just as Europe is uniting, so the West must move toward some kind of union."

What kind of union? Here is a question as vital for the new era as the Act of Chapultepec and Article 51 of the United Nations Charter were for the old.

In this situation, I would propose the immediate formation by the President of the United States of a high-level study and organizational commission, mustering our best parliamentary, legal, financial, military, academic, and other talents, charged with exploring the means of strengthening the cohesion of the North Atlantic nations. This would cooperate with whatever European institutions emerge out of the current NATO trends. The U.S. government's representative on the body would have ambassadorial status and cabinet rank, equivalent to that of our delegate to the United Nations. This group, which might become permanent, might then be charged with missions such as:

· Formulation of common NATO negotiating positions toward the Soviet Union on matters of common concern;

· Formulation of a common NATO trading policy toward the Soviet Union and the satellites, emergent or not;

· Formulation of long-range goals of NATO policy,

including cooperative policies of rendering economic and other forms of assistance to the underdeveloped countries of Asia, Africa and Latin America;

• Formulation of a new partnership concept of nuclear relations for peace as well as deterrence to war.

Canada's former Prime Minister Lester B. Pearson recently said that, "There are, of course, many phases of the relations between NATO members, between the states of this embryonic Atlantic community, which should be conducted in the normal diplomatic way. But in the field of defense and foreign policy, those relations, as I see it, should be centralized and coordinated in a mechanism which in some respects at least would serve the same purpose—and operate in the same way—as a cabinet does in a democratic country. This will not be easy, but it is essential, if NATO is to achieve that cohesion and unity which is necessary for its survival."

I share these views.

Unity in the West implies an act of political creation—comparable to that of our Founding Fathers—and perhaps of even greater originality, daring and devotion. In our time, the challenge leads us, compels us, inspires us, toward the building of our great North Atlantic alliance, our "regional grouping," into a North Atlantic Confederation—looking eventually to a worldwide Union of the Free. And to anybody who would find cause for alarm, or scorn, in such a sweeping concept, I would commend a remembrance of some words that begin, "Hearken not to the voice which petulantly tells you that the form of government recommended for your adoption is a novelty in the political world; that it has never yet had a place in the theories of the wildest projectors; that it rashly attempts what it is impossible to accomplish. No, my countrymen, shut your ears against this unhallowed language." The writer was Madison. He was defending the Constitution of the United States.

There is one final reason for seeing the United States in such a role, and it is deeper than all others, practical or philosophic. It is the fact that our dominant commitment from our very birth as a nation has been to everlasting concern for the individual, his freedom and his dignity.

This is why we were born as a nation—not as an economic convenience or as an imperial adventure. We came into being for the sake of an *idea*: our belief that man should be free to fulfill his unique and individual destiny —a belief based upon our dedicated faith in the brotherhood of all mankind. The nation that was founded in the eighteenth century provided a home—a political structure —in which free men could live a life of such fulfillment.

Yet this, in a real sense, could never be enough. No matter how this nation strove to isolate itself in past generations, it could never suppress or deny an impulse toward the world. In one age, this impulse expressed itself through missionaries; in another age, through philanthropy, medical care, deeds of charity; and, most recently, through massive international aid and assistance.

There is a reason why this impulse has always asserted itself. Our Founding Fathers, obviously, built a home for one nation. Yet the idea to which they and this nation were committed—the idea of human freedom—was, is and can *only* be universal.

We are bound as a people, in the deepest sense, to live by this commitment with a boldness, a confidence, and a clarity of vision matching those who led us to national life.

X

THE MODERN
PRESIDENCY

*The President from time to time may direct the Commission
to—*

*(1) deliver such quantities of fissionable materials or weapons
to the armed forces for such use as he deems necessary in the
interest of the national defense or*

*(2) authorize the armed forces to manufacture, produce or
acquire any equipment or device utilizing fissionable material or
atomic energy as a military weapon.*
                    —The Atomic Energy Act of 1946

The modern Presidency of the United States, as distinct from the traditional concepts of our highest office, is bound up with the survival not only of freedom but of mankind. Yet the very exigencies of the Presidency—not to mention the qualities of common sense and idealism required of the Presidents—set forth a safeguard that is increasingly relevant as we move toward the 1970's and 1980's. The deterrent must continue to deter. The decent respect we pay to the opinions of mankind must continue to be paid. The cold steel of power must ever be deployed to safeguard, never to spoil, the warm glow of hope. Alexander Hamilton, writing in _The Federalist_ in the eighteenth century, defines, in fact, a wholly modern check and balance for the atomic age:

"The process of election affords a moral certainty, that the office of President will never fall to the lot of any man who is not in an eminent degree endowed with the requisite qualifications. Talent for low intrigue, and the little arts of popularity, may alone suffice to elevate a man to the first honors in a single state; but it will require other talents, and a different kind of merit, to establish him in the esteem and confidence of the whole Union, or of so considerable a portion of it as would be necessary to make him a successful candidate for the distinguished office of President of the United States. It will not be too strong to say, that there will be a constant probability of seeing the station filled by characters pre-eminent for ability and virtue."

Professor Clinton Rossiter, who, among most other students of the Presidency, delights in categorizing the thirty-six Presidencies as great, near-great and so on down the line, focuses on a fact of fundamental importance with reference to the hydrogen bomb. He points out that over the first 180 years of our country, not one despot, profligate or scoundrel has made the grade to the White House.

The Presidency, like every other instrument of power

we have created for our use, he says, operates within a grand and durable pattern of private liberty and public morality—which means that it operates successfully only when the President honors the pattern by selecting ends and means that are "characteristically American." The Presidency was, is, and foreseeably will be the most thoroughly American of all institutions.

The Presidency, moreover, is a very significant element of the freedom, security and hope we mean to offer the world during the 1970's and 1980's. As Pierce Butler wrote to a friend in England during the Constitutional Convention in Philadelphia:

"*Entre nous,* I do not believe they (the executive powers granted to the President) would have been so great had not many of the members cast their eyes toward George Washington as President; and shaped their ideas of the Powers to be given a President, by their opinions of his Virtue."

And as Woodrow Wilson, an authority on constitutional government and international law, wrote in the final year of Theodore Roosevelt's tenure of the White House:

"The President can never again be the mere domestic figure he has been throughout so large a part of our history. The nation has risen to the first rank in power and resources. The other nations of the world look askance upon her, half in envy, half in fear, and wonder with a deep anxiety what she will do with her vast strength. Our President must always, henceforth, be one of the great powers of the world, whether he act greatly, or wisely, or not. He must stand always at the front of our affairs, and the office will be as big and as influential as the man who occupies it."

President Woodrow Wilson himself turned out to be as big and as influential as Theodore Roosevelt, especially in social and monetary reform. Yet Wilson's failure to make sense of the Treaty of Versailles and to obtain U.S. membership in his League of Nations is even more relevant to the 1970's and 1980's. He stretched his powers beyond their limits and they snapped. He had failed to recognize the restraints put upon the exercise of the Presidential role at home and overseas. Theodore Roosevelt did not so misconstrue the consensus he drew to his Presidency and, in this respect also, he may be studied as a model, modern national leader. He intervened to head off the outbreak of world war over Venezuela and then Morocco, and he won the Nobel Peace Prize for mediating the Russo-Japanese conflict of 1904–5. But he understood when *not* to intervene, as when he declined to rescue the Armenians from persecution in Turkey. He said:

"It is a literal, physical impossibility to interfere, save in the most guarded manner, under penalty of making this nation ridiculous and of aggravating instead of ameliorating the fate of those for whom we interfere. It could under no conceivable circumstances do good, unless there was an intention to back up the words by an appeal to arms."

This leads me directly to the point that the Presidency's secret strength is its political nature—perhaps this is *the* critical safeguard for the hydrogen stalemate.

The President is the unifying force in our lives. He alone of all our elected officials has the entire people as his constituency, the entire nation as his charge, and he must embody the national will and purpose as Chief Executive and Chief of State.

The President must possess a wide range of abilities: to lead, to persuade, to inspire trust, to attract men of talent, to unite. These abilities must reflect a wide range of characteristics: courage, vision, integrity, intelligence, sense of responsibility, sense of history, sense of humor, warmth, openness, personality, tenacity, energy, determination, drive, perspicacity, idealism, thirst for information, penchant for fact, presence of conscience, comprehension of people and enjoyment of life—plus all the other, nobler virtues ascribed to George Washington under God. And—as was once said in defining the ideal attributes for a federal judge—"it would also help if he has some knowledge of the law."

But the contribution that *political* training brings to American Presidents is a compulsory and often painful education in the democratic process. As Roosevelt wrote to his friend Jacob Riis about his first years in the New York State Legislature: "The men from Erie, from Suffolk, from anywhere, would not work with me. The things I wanted to do I was powerless to accomplish. So I made up my mind there were several other excellent people there with honest opinions of the right. We did not agree in all things, but we did in some, and on those we pulled together."

I might add that as Governor of New York State, I have had precisely, in too many issues to enumerate, a similar experience and a similar education, and these have led to a similar conclusion. I moved from appointive to elective

roles in the public service because I knew that one had
to represent a constituency to accomplish anything of lasting value—to be an "authentic man of the people," as our
Latin American friends would say. I have proven able, I
believe, in my relationship with the New York State Legislature, to heed the views, opinions and concerns of many
men, and, often, to seek the honest compromise. This has
also meant the capacity to distinguish between concession
and capitulation, of course, but as Burke observed, "All
governments, indeed every human benefit and enjoyment,
every virtue and every prudent act, is founded on compromise."

The modern executive must present to the modern legislature the programs he believes to be needed, helpful
and useful, and he must then be generally flexible in ac-
commodating legitimate objections and accepting fair re-
buffs. On the other hand, there is an irreducible core in
any proposition that cannot be compromised, and the
executive must know where this core lies, and fight for his
convictions along the perimeter.

At the Presidential level, all this has infinitely greater
meaning. A true mark of Presidential leadership is a serious awareness of our federal system of government. This
means governmental action not only at the national, but
also at the state and local centers of power. This means
keeping government as close as possible to the people it
is trying to serve and the problems it is trying to solve. It
means a recognition of the fact that each group in our
community may have its special wants, but may not have
special rights, and may have particular needs, but none

have particular privileges. Our unity lies, in its heart, within our commitment to our sovereign belief in the dignity and freedom of the individual. The very last words a free nation expects to hear from its President are: "Tell me where you want me to lead you," or "I'll do anything, if you'll give me a comfortable consensus," or, "I'll show you my bravery—if you assure me of my popularity." Always in our history—but perhaps today more than ever in our history—we need leadership willing to make hard choices and take the tough decisions.

Whenever one mentions "hard choices" and "tough decisions" one must consider, front and center, the Presidency of Harry Truman—and he, too, is in many respects a model, modern President. Perhaps, in retrospect, in our age of refined public opinion polls, the wonder is that President Truman accomplished so much on such a consistently appalling rating. All through the Korea year of 1950, Truman's Gallup Poll rating on "doing a good job" varied from 37 percent to 46 percent—as contrasted to President Eisenhower's and President Kennedy's usual stellar appearances in the fifties, sixties and even seventies—and for Truman this was one of his better years. His low point in his first term, in 1946, was 32 percent. After 1950, his Gallup Polls fluctuated downward from 32 percent to 23 percent. How he was re-elected was a miracle.

Yet President Truman went into office with one of the great, true statements of the White House. He said: "Boys, if you ever pray, pray for me now. When they told me what happened, I felt like the moon, the stars and all the planets had fallen on me."

Harry Truman then decided to reverse President Roosevelt's policy of accommodations with the Kremlin, decided to terminate World War II by dropping two atomic bombs on Japan, decided to contain Soviet expansion into the Mediterranean by offering the Truman Doctrine to Greece and Turkey, decided to help rebuild Western Europe with Marshall Plan transfusions, decided to defend Western Europe and lay the foundations of Western unity by forming the North Atlantic Treaty Organization, decided not to commit the U.S. armed forces to the defense of Nationalist China, decided to respond to the North Korean invasion of South Korea, decided to negotiate the Japanese Peace Treaty and stabilize Northeast Asia.

In domestic affairs, far from being overwhelmed by the moon, the stars and all the planets that fell upon him, he was cocky and assertive and, in 1952, went much too far when he took over the steel mills and was reversed 6–3 by the Supreme Court. In that instance, such was the prestige of the Presidency that Clarence Randall, of Inland Steel Company, in a televised address to the nation, differentiated between Presidential powers and excessive use of them. Randall offers us another lesson today:

"Happily, we still live in a country where a private citizen may look the President in the eye and tell him that he was wrong, but actually, it is not the President of the United States to whom I make answer. It is Harry S. Truman, the man, who last night so far transgressed his oath of office, so far abused the power that is temporarily his, that he must now stand and take it."

President Truman's low Gallup Poll rating even led to a rebirth in modern times of the traditional argument that the dignity of the White House clothes its occupants, that "the office makes the man—even little Harry Truman." But there is another surprising aspect about the Truman Administration, long since forgotten, that is another lesson for the 1970's and 1980's. It is also another sharp comment to be made about the durability of the federal idea. President Truman's leadership—exerted with peculiar force in years of virtually constant crisis—attracted to his Administration a lineup of bipartisan talent rarely seen in our country before or since. Truman's reputation for teamwork has come down to us as "cronyism" and "five percenters" and "corruption in Washington," and there *was* plenty of that, but look at the rest of the lineup: Marshall, Acheson, Lovett, Forrestal, Eisenhower, Dulles, Harriman, Bradley, Hoffman, Bedell Smith, Kennan, Draper, Bohlen, McCloy, Foster, Symington, Douglas, Finletter, Patterson, Clay and, for more than five years, MacArthur. This was the type of attraction of the talents envisaged by the Founding Fathers, as it was also the type of strong Presidency envisaged. Truman left office with another true statement of Presidential aspiration:

"I may not have been one of the great Presidents, but I had a good time trying to be."

On President Truman's desk there reposed the legendary definition of the modern Presidency:

THE BUCK STOPS HERE.

The Presidential powers deriving from constitutional

and precedental origin, from the consent of the governed, under God, today form an imposing roster. The President is chief of state, the uncrowned king, the embodiment of the people's majesty. The President is commander in chief, with power to elevate or demote, deploy or stand easy several millions of armed men and dependent civilians. The President is our chief diplomat, with a virtually personal responsibility for the conduct of our foreign relations, and he is the chief watchman of our private enterprise economy. The President is the head of the civil service—more than 2,900,000 people—and he has the power of pardon and reprieve over federal and military prisoners. He is a prime mover of legislation and he submits his proposals to Congress and vetoes proposals of which he disapproves, although this veto can of course be overridden, and although he does not possess the cherished "item veto" which Presidents traditionally demand and are refused.

The President is the chief appointment-maker to the federal judiciary—and thus serves as a check on that check and balance—appointing more than 450 federal judges, all the way up to the Chief Justice of the United States. He also has power of appointment for more than 200 officers of various regulatory commissions, with Senate approval. He is the leader of his political party, the voice of the national will, and is subject to removal only at the end of his term, by impeachment, or by death.

The President by custom also selects the Vice-President, although this is a reflection of the leverage he holds over his party's national convention, and he may use his man as he chooses. Even today, the Vice-President is rarely able to emerge as a national leader in his own right, even though we have progressed far from the days when Mr. Dooley urged Theodore Roosevelt not to go down in a submarine—"Well, you really shouldn't do it, unless you take (Vice-President) Fairbanks with you." Woodrow Wilson's Thomas R. Marshall said that he was "conscious of all that goes on, but has no part of it," and what the country needed was a good five-cent cigar. President Eisenhower said later that, "I personally believe the Vice-President of the United States should never be a nonentity. I believe he should be used. I believe he should have a very useful job."

None of these Presidential powers comes even close, however, by terms of relative measurement of the consequences, to the new atomic power. Whose finger is on the trigger, whose hand is poised over the button, is no mere electioneering oratory. The development of the hydrogen bomb in 1954 set in motion the deterrent buildup on both sides of the Cold War that held within it the possible destruction of most forms of life. Today the Presidency is moving into a new dimension—and the Presidential qualities seek redefinition. These require some spelling out—and I will draw upon my own experiences of the way two of our Presidents handled various aspects of the strategic balance.

My first intimate experience of the Presidency in the hydrogen age came when I was transferred to President Eisenhower's staff in the White House in December 1954, to serve as Special Assistant to the President for Foreign Affairs. My mission was to give "advice and assistance in

the development of increased understanding and cooperation among all peoples." This led swiftly to the creation
of a Planning Coordination Group intended to serve as a
review procedure for overseas economic and information
programs. The problem we faced, as I saw it, was the
other side of the coin of the very necessary development
of the hydrogen bomb. The reports that poured in to us
from everywhere in the world showed that many feared or
resented this deployment and did not understand our motivation. There were shrill cries—and reasoned arguments
—that the bomb should be banned and our bases dismantled. Through the Planning Coordination Group, I
began to prepare a counterstatement everybody could believe: that the United States was seeking peace. The point
to be presented to President Eisenhower, on the eve of his
summit conference with the Russians at Geneva, was that
we should demonstrate our peaceful purposes in full view
of the whole world.

The Planning Coordination Group held a seminar of
military, financial, political, academic and other "think-
tank" authorities at Quantico, Va., on the subject of
nuclear disarmament. All of these men were cleared for
top-secret information, and out of the meetings came a
proposal for mutual aerial inspection of the U.S. and the
U.S.S.R. This was the genesis of the "Open Skies" plan
that was to make history. When I presented the idea to
President Eisenhower in a one-page memorandum, he
icked up the telephone, and told Secretary of State
Dulles, "Foster, here's an idea."

A few days later, I sat down with Eisenhower and

Dulles, and said, "I believe, Mr. President, that you should make a pronouncement that will reassure the world as to the peaceful intentions of the United States. It is important that you destroy the idea some people have that the United States is a warmonger with an atomic bomb. You can be sure the Russians will attempt to make themselves out as leading the search for peace. The Russian argument will be propaganda, but it will be important, psychologically." Dulles was skeptical, but President Eisenhower directed that an "open skies" task force of experts be held in reserve in Paris while he went to Geneva. These included the Chairman of the Joint Chiefs of Staff, Admiral Arthur W. Radford, Deputy Defense Secretary Robert B. Anderson, and Special Assistant for Disarmament Harold Stassen, in addition to myself. We showed the idea to General Alfred M. Gruenther, then commanding general of NATO, and he, too, liked "open skies."

President Eisenhower personally decided after several days of cold-war sparring and bargaining at Geneva that the summit was getting nowhere. He also decided that the Russians were making headway in their insistence that we were the warmongers of the new era. So he called us down to Switzerland, and laid the "open skies" plan on the conference table before the Russians. "I propose," he said, "that we take a practical step; that we begin an arrangement very quickly as between ourselves, immediately." The rest of the story is well-known and I will summarize it briefly. The President's statement at Geneva was interrupted by a tremendous clap of thunder and the lights in the conference room flickered, adding a note of high drama to the "open skies" proposal. And although Russia's Premier Nikolai Bulganin appeared briefly to like the idea, the irrepressible Nikita S. Khrushchev would have none of it.

President Eisenhower thus "won" the Geneva Conference by paying respect to the opinions of mankind without in one iota diminishing our defenses. President Eisenhower was also presenting an idea that was, in itself, ahead of its time: "open skies" might well be a basic technique of détente between East and West for the 1970's and 1980's.

My second experience of the Presidency in the hydrogen age came eight years later, while I was in the midst of my second term as Governor of New York. President John F. Kennedy and British Prime Minister Harold Macmillan, among others, were concluding their epic quest for a treaty formally banning nuclear tests in the atmosphere and the matter was up for ratification in the Senate. The pressures of the moment were quite exceptional, and the few who sought clarification of the treaty, who sought clear definitions of the safeguards, were open to heavy political attack. I resolved to take my own stand and take whatever lumps came my way. I put out a formal statement of support for the test-ban treaty with important qualifications:

"Because the treaty is so identified with the hopes and yearnings for peace, and because the prestige of the United States has already been so solemnly committed to the treaty, I believe that the United States Senate should consent to its ratification. At the same time, I think the Senate should so advise the President about its concern regarding the treaty itself and the measures it considers necessary to maintain the defense of freedom. This in my opinion should include the following elements:

"1. The Senate should make clear that the treaty is ratified with the understanding that certain ambiguous language in Article I does not prohibit the use of nuclear weapons to repel aggression anywhere.

"2. The Administration should take every feasible step to preserve the ability of our military establishment to deter and defeat Communist aggression against free peoples everywhere. Specifically, there should be a national commitment that . . . we must at all times be prepared, able and willing to use nuclear weapons to repel aggression, alone or together with our allies. . . . We will utilize to the full the possibilities of underground nuclear testing for continued weapons development. . . . We will vigorously pursue research and development . . . of our weapons laboratories . . . and in the vital area of anti-missile defense and . . . we will prepare a series of standby tests in the atmosphere for the contingency of cancellation of the treaty.

"3. The Administration should take positive and immediate steps to strengthen the unity and vitality of NATO.

"4. The United States should take effective steps to avoid being caught short again by Soviet duplicity as occurred when Russia broke the nuclear test moratorium in 1961. These steps should include the installation of a space surveillance system which would detect nuclear testing in outer space.

"5. The United States should vigorously pursue the beneficial and peaceful uses of atomic energy. The Senate should make clear its understanding that the language of the treaty does not prohibit nuclear explosions for peaceful uses, under adequate safeguards, for such purposes as the construction of another Panama Canal."

Five years have passed, and the nuclear test-ban treaty has stood, and so have our underground testing programs, our space surveillance, and our weapons development continued to protect our people from surprise attack and from an undue tilting of the balance of power. I would reiterate today my statement of 1963. I would stress once again that our national idealism, implicit in "Open Skies," is in being, in measure, due to the effectiveness of our defenses. In this area of survival, there may be no second chances.

Professor Clinton Rossiter avers in his classic *The American Presidency* that the chief executive office has to some extent been "institutionalized" to meet similar crisis situations at home and abroad. This is a question of rising importance and opportunity, provided that the new institutions are efficient and useful and not merely a bureaucratic extension. In recent years, the Presidency has acquired an Executive Office of the President, a White House Office, a National Security Council, a Scientific Adviser to the President, a Council of Economic Advisers, an Office of Defense Mobilization and, above all, the Bureau of the Budget, with its rapidly expanding money powers and influence over all segments of our federal government and national life.

In *The Public Interest,* the visiting British political writer Henry Fairlie, the inventor of the term "The Establishment," wrote not long ago that, "Climbing the steps of the Executive Office Building to visit the Bureau of the Budget is very like what it must have been to call on the scarcely known men who constituted the pertinacious bureaucracy of Henry II. At any moment, when they talk of Commerce, or Agriculture, or Health, Education and Welfare as if these were part of a rebellious ecclesiastical or lay baronage, one expects to hear the cry 'Who will rid me of this turbulent priest,' and one would not in the least be surprised if five knights rode immediately down Pennsylvania Avenue to butcher the department heads in the sanctuary of their departments."

Fairlie doubted that the Presidency was becoming institutionalized, however, because the Presidents tended to shape their machinery to their own purposes. He quoted Theodore Sorensen's *Kennedy* to this end:

"From the outset, Kennedy abandoned the notion of a collective, institutionalized Presidency. He ignored Eisenhower's farewell recommendation to create a First Secretary of Government to oversee all foreign affairs agencies. He abandoned the practice of the Cabinet's and the National Security Council's making group decisions like corporate boards of directors. He abolished the White House practice of White House staff meetings and weekly cabinet meetings. He abolished the pyramid-structure of the White House staff, the Staff Secretary, the Cabinet Secretariat, the NSC Planning Board and the Operations Coordinating Board, all of which imposed, in his view, needless paperwork and machinery between the President and his responsible officers. . . . He relied instead on informal meetings and direct contacts—on a personal White House staff, the Budget Bureau and ad hoc task forces, to probe and define issues for his decision."

Fairlie finally commented that President Kennedy reminded him of Justinian, and he quoted the article on Justinian in the *Encyclopaedia Britannica,* which had been composed by Lord Bryce: "Justinian's age was quite unequal in intellect to so vast an undertaking as the fusing on scientific principles into one organic whole of the entire law of the empire." These are words of warning, worth addressing to the new men of our own age, says Fairlie, and I would answer, yes, of course, and this is precisely why we have devised a federal system and now seek a partnership of all the talents to solve the problems that perplex us. The federal idea will make it possible for us to create new opportunities and take action to grasp them.

There is a significant addition to be made to the "institutionalizing" of the Presidency, and I am advancing it for consideration. I believe there should be a new federal mechanism devised to assist the President in the conduct of foreign relations. We usually think of the State Department as the responsible body in this regard, and yet several other agencies of government are deeply involved in the making and implementing of foreign policy, most notably the Department of Defense, the Central Intelligence Agency, the U.S. Treasury, the Agency for International Development, the U.S. Information Agency, and the Bureau of the Budget. The new mechanism would serve among other things to coordinate all these operations.

I also believe that the President's effectiveness in domestic affairs could be substantially increased by the appointment of an Executive Assistant to the President— heading a new Office of Executive Management. The Executive Assistant would control five key staff functions in developing, coordinating and executing Administration policies: budgeting, program planning, legislative relations, organization and management, and, lastly, personnel management. This office would solve the problem, hopefully, of chaos in the White House in which shifting staff assignments are patched together on an ad hoc basis to bring the Chief Executive the options he needs for decision.

I also believe that the President needs vastly improved systems of information. We need to use computers to store the factual mass of cables, reports and briefing papers that inundate the White House and paralyze the office of the Chief Executive. Computers may be programmed to store, summarize, retrieve and display in orderly, comprehensible, graphic format the basic data of world events ranging from the capacity of Japanese oil tankers to the location of orbiting debris from space shots to the infant mortality rates in the Chicago slums. The President badly needs objective information—pure fact, whenever possible, and not a cabinet member's two-week-old recollection of a bureau chief's impressions of an ambassador's memorandum sent two months previously.

The computer can help develop early warning signals, notifying the White House of indices of incoming crises in advance. From such a sophisticated information system —of men and machines—the President will be able to obtain the data and criteria upon which he can measure his action-options while he is in the midst of his decision-making process.

I also believe that the President should require the major departments to follow the practice of the Defense Department in developing five-year projections of programs and goals—and that he should create a new system of objective measurement of the effectiveness of his policies, utilizing the newest evaluation techniques.

I wholly believe that the Presidential leadership—in this atomic age—must have specific strengths if it is to heal our nation and inspire our people and maintain our peace and freedom. It must have the courage to make stern decisions. It must profoundly understand our federal system of shared powers and partnership. It must believe in the private enterprise economy. It must sensitively know the revolutionary, changing times in which we live. It must expertly manage the government. It must intelligently set the priorities and never forget that we cannot do everything at once. It must speak—*one* voice, *straight* talk—to all the people, all the time. It must represent a united nation.

It is with this conviction that I seek the Presidency of the United States—and I stress the word *United*. I deeply believe and feel this commitment to national unity—and never was it more sorely needed.

Wherever we look upon this earth, the opportunities take shape even within the problems: Peace with honor in Vietnam. Security for friendly nations in Asia. The survival of Israel and a stop to Soviet expansion in the Middle East. Unity in the West. New lives for the hungry of Asia, Africa and Latin America. Civil rights and human rights at home as well as abroad. One voice, straight talk, to all peoples. Destruction of the slums, and the creation of new jobs. An end to the riots—and the downfall of those who preach violence. The fight against crime—and the rehabilitation of offenders to useful lives. The right of men and women everywhere to decent medical care. Better education for the young. Fulfillment for women in more meaningful roles. Awareness of the arts. Protection of our natural resources, clean air and pure water. A new concept of leisure. A rising tide of prosperity. A rising belief that peace is relevant not in soft, meaningless generalities but in hard specifics of shared interests. Arms controls. A true sense of neighborliness and dignity among men and continents of all colors. Equality of all men under God.

The task—the opportunity—is truly momentous.

The need is for the unifier who can reach into the problems to find and secure new hope.

Many generations ago, Benjamin Franklin pointed across the hall of the Constitutional Convention at Philadelphia to the golden half-sun engraved on the back of Washington's chair, and he remarked: "Now, at length, I have the happiness to know that it is a rising, not a setting, sun." And so today, when a single fireball can light the fires of ten thousand suns, we need to reaffirm our faith in America.

These are the outlines of my own belief—my own vision —of our future.

These things *can be done*.